The Dragon and the Lamb

The Dragon and the Lamb

Wayne Dehoney

BROADMAN PRESS
Nashville, Tennessee

Acknowledgments

I am indebted to many persons for their counsel, encouragement, and assistance.

Foremost is Britt E. Towery, Jr., of the Cooperative Services Foundation. Towery's excellent book *The Churches of China* was a valuable resource. His extensive experience in today's China, his contacts with religious leaders and his understanding of the dynamics at work in the churches were invaluable to me.

The many Chinese Christians quoted in the book, Mr. Han Wenzao, Dr. C. K. Chang, Mr. Li Shou-bao, other pastors and lay persons, all gave freely of their time in numerous interviews.

Other Chinese believers are unnamed or deliberately disguised with fictional names or variations in circumstances. They revealed in confidence opinions and intimate details of personal experiences. I have kept their trust by hiding their identity while faithfully telling their story.

I am indebted to Lewis Myers, Harlan Spurgeon, John Jonsson, Cornelia Leavell, Barbara Chafin, Bryan Glass, others who read my manuscript and helped with style, facts, and the Chinese language.

Special credit is due Ms. Mildred Snow, my personal secretary for thirty-five years. Although in retirement, she readily accepted the challenge of *The Dragon and the Lamb* and compiled massive notes, edited, and typed numerous rewrites.

Most important of all has been my traveling companion, not only in China, but also on life's greatest journey for almost a half century, my wife Lealice, the light of my life and the love of my heart to whom I dedicate this book.

The Dragon . . .
>Beneficent amphibian deity of Oriental mythology . . .
>Ageless symbol of greatness, royalty, power . . .
>For two thousand years the emperor of China sat on
>>a dragon throne and ruled the Land of the Dragon.

and the Lamb . . .
>Slain from the foundations of the world . . .
>That taketh away the sins of all peoples . . .
>And He shall reign forever and ever.

The Story of the Rebirth of Christianity in the New China.

Contents

Introduction

If a book were written entitled *China Today,* it would probably be out of date by the time it was published, so rapid and surprising are the changes taking place in the People's Republic of China.

For twenty-seven years the "Great Helmsman" Mao Zedong (Tse-tung)[1] and his chief colleague, Zhou Enlai, charted a predictable direction for the newly formed government of China. With an unrelenting hand Mao guided the new nation on an orthodox Marxist course, claiming to be purer in doctrine than even Russian Communism.[2]

Then in 1976 both Mao and Zhou died. Even in his wildest imaginations, neither ever expected the changes that would take place in China during the next decade: the undoing of the deification of the Socialist pantheon, Marx, Lenin, Stalin, and even Mao; the repudiation of the most cherished economic tenets of Communism because they were "irrelevant" to the needs of contemporary China; the invention of a new word and a new Sinoized economic system, "socialistic-capitalism"; the plunge toward an open society oriented to the West; the steady restoration of many basic human rights; and all this with a leader, Deng Xiaoping, who was twice exiled by Mao for "heresy and counter-revolutionary ideas."

One of the most astounding changes has been the reemergence of evangelical Christianity in form and with vigor explainable only in terms of "the miraculous workings of the power of God."

This dramatic story first began to unfold for me in 1978 when I entered China leading a group of Christian educators and ministers. I have since returned to China a number of times.

While working on this book for several years, I discovered that the last chapter of this story cannot be written. What that chapter will be is as problematic as has been every other chapter of this continually developing and unfinished story. The future defies premeditation and prediction. Nothing in the present is absolute or final. But perhaps the last chapter has already been written in another Book that declares, "The kingdoms of this world are become the kingdoms of our Lord" (Rev. 11:15).

I tell my story as a developing drama seen through the eyes of a tourist-visitor. My style is narrative and episodical rather than critical in order that the reader may not only "learn" about China but also "experience" China. I tell of a new China: her exciting cities, memorable sights, friendly people, and, above all, devoted Christian believers and dynamic churches.

This is the untold story of the Dragon and the Lamb, Christianity in socialist China, where believers are increasing twice as fast as the birth rate.[3]

Notes

1. In 1978 China adopted a new system of spelling. Throughout this book I will use the new spellings. The first time a personal or place name is used the old spelling, if known and different, will be in parentheses.

2. *The Wilson Quarterly,* Autumn, 1980. Article by Dick Wilson "Mao and the Russians," p. 113. Mao called Khrushchev a "turnip communist" (that is, red only on the outside) and opened an all-out attack on Soviet-style communism in 1960.

3. Address by Bishop K. H. Ting before the Fourth National Conference on Religious Work, meeting in Beijing in August of 1986.

1

The Dragon Is Awake

President Richard Nixon said at a dinner, "Our two peoples hold the future of the world in our hands. We can build a new world! If we succeed in working together, generations in the years ahead will look back and thank us for this meeting."[1]

It was March 20, 1972, in the Great Hall of the People in Beijing (Peking). Premier Zhou Enlai was the host on Nixon's epochal visit to the People's Republic of China.

Thirteen years later, Nixon, as a private citizen, made his fourth visit to China. He told Beijing University students, "Napoleon said, 'China, there's a sleeping giant! Don't awaken her! Because when you do, she will move the world.'" He continued, "Well, China is awake today! And with the help of your generation, China will lead the world in the paths of peace and progress."[2]

The Dragon is not only alive and awake but also has abandoned the isolationism that cut the Chinese people off from the rest of the world for centuries. This giant, with more than one billion people, is joining the world family of nations. China's new openness and turn outward to the West may well be the most significant single event of the twentieth century!

"How does one grasp the concept of a billion people?" I asked Southern Baptist missiologist Lewis Meyers.

"Simply imagine all the people in the world marching by you single file," he replied. "Every fifth person is Chinese!" The potential impact of a new China on all aspects of world society stirs our imagination beyond measure. Imagine the lucrative market of a billion consumers for the manufactured goods of the industrialized West! On the other hand, imagine the impact on the balance of trade when a modernized China with a limitless force of cheap labor becomes a producer nation! Imagine the political and military prowess of a modernized Chinese army with nuclear capabilities. Remember several years ago, China fought the United States to a standstill on the desolate hills of North Korea.

The Christian's Concern

As Christians, many of us have special emotions concerning China. For decades China was the grandest object of our missionary concern. As children, we prayed for the people in China. China was the social concern of our generation as Ethiopia has been for today's world. Our parents admonished at mealtime, "Don't waste food. Remember, little children are starving in China." We heard missionaries tell of "fields white unto harvest." We read about Robert Morrison, Lottie Moon, Hudson Taylor, Bill Wallace—valiant missionaries who died serving Christ in China. It is difficult for today's generation to understand our burden of memories and the emotional investment that produced this love-serve-pity syndrome about China.

The victory of the Communists and the departure of missionaries in 1949 devastated us. We felt the Antichrist had won! But only for the moment. We were assured by the John Foster Dulles foreign policy of our nation that the "true China was on the island of Taiwan." It was only a matter of time before Chiang Kai shek would cross the Taiwan Strait and free the mainland. Then we could again send missionaries and get on with the business of evangelizing China.

Now, thirty-six years later, three realities have emerged.

First, there will be no victorious military liberation force from Taiwan.

Second the Communist revolution and Mao Zedong's twenty-seven-year rule irreversibly changed China. Almost a decade under the regime of Deng Xiaoping continued to bring radical changes in the new China. We cannot return to the China of yesterday!

Third, the West will not be sending missionaries to the new China, certainly not the same kind and in the same manner as in the past.

However, this does not mean that China is closed to Christianity. My conviction is that the doors, instead of being closed, are really off their hinges.

My purpose is to explore this premise with you. To do so, we must first look briefly at the land, people, and history to better understand the dynamics at work in present-day China.

The Land

"Dig a well straight down through the earth and you will come out in China." This is probably the first recollection we have as children about this mysterious land on the other side of the globe. China is slightly larger than the United States. Three-fourths of the country is made up of wind-swept deserts and barren, precipitous mountains. Only one-fourth of the land is tillable. China must feed one person with one fourth acre of tillable soil compared to the U.S. ratio of two acres per person.

Geographically there are three Chinas, like a three-tiered staircase. The upper step, "the top of the world," is in the southwest, the provinces of Xizang (Tibet), Gansu, and part of Sichuan. This desolate region has hundreds of mountains over 15,000 feet high (the highest in the U.S. is Mount McKinley, 20,320 feet, in Alaska). China has ten mountains over 26,000 feet high. Chomolungma Fang (Mount Everest), with an altitude of 29,028 feet, is the world's highest mountain.

Step 2 is the 6,000-foot level, the provinces of northwestern and central China. The lowest step, curving like a belt to the south and east, is made up of mountains, mostly 3,000 feet and under, and cut by river deltas that run out to the sea. This is the place most of the foreign tourists visit today and where most of the Chinese live. In a vast rural triangle bounded by Xi'an, Shanghai, and Beijing, the population density is 520 people per square mile, about ten times the U.S. average.

The People

The Chinese are the only major race of people who are indigenous to their land. The rest of the world's people immigrated in a distant past to the places where they now live. The Chinese have always been there. The Chinese believe that the 350,000-year-old fossil remains of Peking man, found in a cave near Beijing in 1927, are those of a direct ancestor. Today, the Han Chinese constitute 94 percent of China's population. There are fifty-five national minorities scattered throughout China that constitute the other 6 percent.

An Ancient Culture

The Chinese are justly proud of a history, culture, and civilization that goes back five thousand years! The Emperor Yao lounged in silken robes on a dragon throne on the banks of the Hwang Ho (Yellow River) while Abraham was dwelling in tents. From antiquity, the Chinese have possessed an almost arrogant sense of superiority and self-sufficiency. China called herself "The Middle Kingdom," the center of the world, and even of the universe. All outsiders were barbarians, foreign and inferior.

This great civilization gave the world many remarkable inventions and innovations: gunpowder, the compass, the sailing ship, the printing press, paper, commercial banking, and civil administration.

Portions of the Great Wall were built two hundred years before the birth of Christ.

While our ancestors in Western Europe dressed in skins and lived in caves, China was producing the great philosophers, Lao-tzu, Confucius, Mo Ti, and Mencius.

Christianity Enters China

An unsubstantiated legend has the apostle Thomas preaching the gospel in China in the first century. The first documented record of Christianity in China is that of Christians from Syria who established a mission in Xi'an, the ancient capital of China, in the seventh century. Two centuries later all evidence of their work had vanished, remembered only by the Nestorian Tablet in the Provincial Museum in Xi'an.

Two hundred years before Columbus discovered America, Marco Polo visited China. A Roman Catholic missionary, John de Montecorvino, followed. In less than a century political upheaval put an end to that mission and all Christians were expelled.

Two centuries later, Ruggieri and Ricci, Italian Jesuit priests, entered China. This time the Christian work flourished. In the next 150 years, 500 Catholic missionaries entered China. Again political upheaval caused all foreigners to be expelled, Chinese Christians were persecuted, and China was closed.

Protestant Missions

In 1807 Robert Morrison was the first Protestant missionary to enter China. On the voyage out, the ship's captain asked the indomitable Scotchman if he seriously expected "to make an impression on the idolatry of the Chinese empire." Steeped in a strong Calvinistic faith, Morrison replied, "No, Sir. But I expect God will."

Morrison went to Guangzhou (Canton) as an employee of a trading company. He lived and worked under the most austere circumstances, finding housing in a French warehouse. He dressed in Chinese garb to avoid notice. Morrison pursued the study of the Chinese language with a native who carried a poison pill in his pocket. The Chinese tutor was prepared to commit suicide if he were caught violating the emperor's stringent orders against instructing foreigners.

Concrete evidence of God's blessings on Morrison's work came painfully and slowly. Seven years passed before Morrison baptized his first convert. He baptized a total of only ten converts in the first twenty-five years. Though his gains numerically were meager, Morrison laid an enduring foundation for the future expansion of the Christian work in China. His contributions included the production of a massive English-Chinese dictionary, a Chinese translation of the Bible, and a limitless number of tracts, pamphlets, and catechisms. He founded a dispensary and a college. In addition, he preached and taught every day of his life in China.

In the years to follow all the principal Protestant denominations of Europe and America sent missionaries. They spread the work into every province, founding churches, schools, and hospitals. The largest single enterprise was the nondenominational China Inland Mission founded by J. Hudson Taylor. By 1900 there were 1,500 Protestant missionaries in China. By 1925 the missionary total peaked with 8,000.

Gunboat Evangelism

During the 1800s, the ruling dynasty (the Manchus) tried to resist all foreign influence and keep out all foreigners. But the West was in a heyday of colonial expansion, hungry for raw materials, goods, and markets. When the Chinese government refused to open seaports to foreign trade, the Europeans sent gunboats and soldiers in to establish "open trade."

The most frequently cited example of ruthless colonialism is the infamous Opium War. The British had a balance of payments problem! China sold the West huge amounts of silk, spices, and tea but bought little from the West. The result was that the British had a trade deficit and China had a silver surplus. The British controlled the world supply of Bengal opium in India and were looking for a market. Their plan was to export Indian opium to China, reverse the flow of silver, and complete the cycle of trade.

The Chinese emperor bitterly resisted. The opium trade was declared illegal. In retaliation, British gunboats bombarded the harbor of Guangzhou and took the city. A reluctant Qing government signed an open trade agreement with the West and opium flowed freely into China, addicting millions.

A rider to the open trade treaty stated, "The principles of the Christian religion . . . are recognized as teaching men to do good . . . those who quietly teach and profess these doctrines shall not be harassed or persecuted on account of their faith," and all such persons who "teach and practice the principles of Christianity shall in no wise be interfered with or molested."

To the missionaries this treaty, at first, seemed to be a great boon to their work. To the resentful Chinese, however, it was "gunboat evangelism," and was bitterly resented. Later a discerning missionary wrote, "The Chinese themselves bracket opium and missionaries as the twin curses of the country." This perception persists even today.[3] A prominent Chinese church leader recently said, "Protestant Christianity was forced upon China in the salvos of gunboats through the intrigues of merchants . . . and unequal treaties."[4]

Antimissionary Riots

The latter part of the nineteenth century was marked by great unrest throughout China. There were numerous antiforeign riots, missionary massacres, and international incidents.

The Boxer Rebellion, an aborted attempt on the part of fanatical young people to throw off foreign domination, was perhaps the most violent. Vast amounts of foreign-owned property were destroyed. Thousands were tortured. One hundred thirty-five missionaries, fifty-two children, and an estimated sixteen thousand Chinese Christians were murdered.

The foreign powers retaliated by imposing huge indemnities upon China and claiming territorial rights. Adding to the bitter defeat in a war with her archenemy, Japan, in 1895, China's ultimate humiliation and final breakup was now at hand. Germany annexed Qingdao (Jiaozhou Bay) and extracted railroad, mining, and trading rights in Shandong (Shantung) Province on the northeast coast. Russia forced an unequal lease on Lushun (opposite Korea). France established her authority in Zhanjiang (on Kwangchow Bay) in south China. England acquired Weihai on the northeast coast and the Kowloon peninsula opposite Hong Kong, to the south. A ring of foreign concessions along the coast hung like a noose around the neck of a subjugated China.

China in This Century

At the turn of this century the situation inside China was desperate. Opium addiction had become the social curse of the masses. Peasants lived as animals, uneducated and without the benefits of modern culture or civilization. They balanced on the knife's edge of survival, often eating grass and roots. Floods and droughts triggered famines in which millions died like flies.

The country was divided and ruled by ruthless warlords and oppressive landowners. The three-hundred-year-old corrupt Manchu Dynasty was dying. Foreign colonial powers occupied her land and exploited her resources. There was stagnation, decay, despair, and hopelessness among the poor in the cities and peasants in the countryside.

Out of the ferment at home and exploitation from abroad came the cascading events of the twentieth century.

On October 10, 1911 China's great day of freedom dawned. A revolutionary force took Wuhan, a city in central China. Three months later the Republic of China was established in Nanjing with Dr. Sun Yatsen as president.

But the provincial and local warlords were not easily dislodged. The country remained divided for the next fifteen years. In 1926, Chiang Kaishek, who later married a sister of Sun Yatsen's wife, organized an army and marched north to unify the Republic. The Nationalist regime had come.

The Communists

In the meantime Communism, as a second major political force, was taking root in China. Chiang's regime was greatly weakened by corruption and brutality. His popularity with the Chinese people further declined because of his alliance with and dependence upon the Western powers. The Communist party was picking up strong support from students and the peasant classes.

In 1934 Chiang set out to dislodge the Communists from their political bases throughout China. His troops numbered six hundred thousand. Victorious in this campaign, Chiang determined to exterminate the Communists. The Nationalists drove the dwindling Red Army westward, sending them on the epic "Long March." Only four thousand soldiers survived the six-thousand mile trek across China. The decimated army finally regrouped in the safety of caves and mountains on the northern frontier in Shaanxi Province. The Long March is one of the most amazing feats in the annals of military history.

On the Long March a new leader emerged. He was Mao Zedong, a peasant-born revolutionary from Hunan Province in south China. With a nucleus of hardened, disciplined soldiers, at the end of World War II, Mao began the drive eastward to do battle with the Nationalists, gathering recruits and support from the peasants along the way.

The Red Army swept all in front of them and reached Beijing in the fall of 1949. On October 1, 1949 the soldiers of the victorious army

filled Beijing's Tien'anmen Square as the revolutionary leader, Mao Zedong, declared the establishment of the People's Republic of China.
Chiang Kaishek and his Nationalist forces were ousted from central and
south China and ultimately fled to Taiwan.

The Great Helmsman

Mao took the helm of a war-weary nation bitterly divided, with its
economy in total disarray, the currency collapsed, and inflation running
wild. Mao took charge with ruthless authority, emotionless decisive-
ness, and unrelenting warfare on all antirevolutionary influences.

In a drive to renounce all things foreign, the new government moved
quickly. Persons considered incompatible or hostile to the revolutionary
regime were to be reeducated or eradicated. Foreign missionaries' activities were restricted. They were denounced as agents of Western impe-
rialism. They were ill-treated, many were imprisoned, and some were
executed. In the end all foreign missionaries either left voluntarily or
were expelled. The era of the evangelization of China by the Christian
West came to an end.

Churches remained open under Chinese leadership, but the pastors
and the members were harassed and placed under constant surveillance
and suspicion; many were persecuted. Under this pressure, church attendance dwindled. Congregations were consolidated by government order and vacated church properties were turned into factories and
warehouses.

Having expelled the foreigners and appropriated their property and
institutions, Mao's first domestic objective was land reform. He ousted
the landlords, many of whom were tried by "people's courts" and sum-
marily executed. Mao confiscated the land, livestock, and farm imple-
ments and declared all property collectively owned.

Then came the "three-anti" movement—anticorruption, antiwaste,
and antibureaucracy. This program was to break the stranglehold of the
government bureaucrats who had held power in Chinese life for thousands of years. It took Mao fifteen years to do this!

In 1958 came the "great leap forward," Mao's calculated effort to
transform China overnight into a modern industrial power. However, his

scheme of backyard furnaces for steel production and small-scale peasant-run factories failed miserably.

The most disastrous venture of the Mao years came with his Cultural Revolution. When Mao thought that the party structure and intellectuals were closing in around him, he faced the choice of surrendering power or smashing the structure. He decided to attack the structure!

In 1966 Mao approved the organizing of the Red Guards. Millions of teenagers were transported to Beijing to be indoctrinated to the point of fanaticism and unleased upon a startled government bureaucracy and an innocent public. In the ten years that followed, radical teenage gangs roamed the streets throughout China, wrecking the structures of orderly society, the government, the schools, the courts, and the religious institutions.

Mao gave the Red Guards the goal to destroy the four olds—old ideas, old culture, old habits, old customs. Their first targets were the intellectuals, the educated upper class, the professionals, the religious, and educational institutions. Chaos reigned as these fanatical and undisciplined hordes of millions ravaged the country. Churches were closed, and pastors and church members suffered greatly. As the Cultural Revolution was burning itself out, Mao Zedong died on September 9, 1976.

Mao's Legacy

Mao, the Great Helmsman, had changed the course of Chinese history, a course that had been set through two thousand years of imperial reign. He had left an indelible mark on the annals of mankind. He must be regarded as one of the important figures of history. Mao and his revolution changed China. When he died, no foreign powers occupied her soil. A strong central government united the sprawling provinces and the scattered people of China. The brutal warlords, who for centuries had fragmented the country into warring fiefdoms, were gone. Famine that periodically devastated vast sections of China had been eliminated. Chinese agriculture was producing enough to feed the people. Unscrupulous landowners, bandits, criminals, prostitutes, and beggars had been reeducated or eradicated.

History will make the moral judgment on the price that was paid in violence and the sacrifice of lives and human liberties to achieve these goals. But there is no question that Mao, the revolutionary, tore down the old structures of a long-established society. He burned and cleared the ground on which to build a new China.

The New Leadership

As Mao's power had waned in the later years, his widow, the vitriolic onetime movie actress, Jiang Qing, attempted to assume power as one of the Gang of Four. This group held power for only a brief time before they were deposed.

Into the leadership vacuum stepped Deng Xiaoping, a most unlikely successor to Mao Zedong.

Deng made the Long March (1934-1936) at Mao's side and was a compatriot with Zhou Enlai. In 1956 Deng was general secretary of the Chinese Communist party.

Deng opposed Mao's rigid method of ruling in 1966 and became one of the first victims of the Cultural Revolution. Young Red Guards dragged Deng from his apartment in Beijing, put a dunce cap on his head, and paraded him through the street. He was exiled to house arrest in a distant province, where he worked at menial tasks for nine years. His wife and family were also persecuted. His eldest son was thrown from an upper-story window and was paralyzed for life.

Deng Xiaoping is a striking contrast to Mao. Deng stands only four feet eleven inches tall compared to the overpowering six-foot hulk of Chairman Mao. Mao was a ruthless revolutionary. Deng is an experienced politician and a successful administrator.

Mao was a hard-line doctrinaire Marxist with great stress on ideology; Deng is a resolute pragmatist. He is no respecter of precedents. Efficiency and success override ideology. Deng once shocked party dogmatists by declaring, "What does it matter if a cat is white or black, so long as it catches rats?"

Mao was an isolationist and a nativist. He preached self-reliance by shutting out the rest of the world. Mao dropped the Bamboo Curtain around China for twenty-seven years. Deng, on the other hand, is turned outward to the West. On Deng's visit to the United States in 1979, he captured the fancy of the American public by wearing a cowboy hat and standing for the photographers between Houston Rockets basketball players almost twice his height.

In an interview with Encyclopedia Britannica's Frank Gibney, Deng said that he was launching a vast program of "four modernizations: Industry, Agriculture, Science and Technology, and National Defense." Deng called his program a "new revolution to provide the people with a better and happier life. During the past 30 years we did some stupid things . . . 'The Gang of Four' tried to edge China off its true course. They even had a slogan: 'We would prefer a poor society under socialism to a rich society under capitalism.' This is absurd! The 'Gang of Four' put the Chinese people in mental straitjackets, stifling their native wisdom and creative talent. We wish to strengthen democracy in our country."[5]

In a race against time (he was seventy-four years old when he took over) Deng is out to change China. He is modeling after and turning to the successful capitalistic nations, primarily the United States and Japan for help.

At the time of this writing, Deng has been in power for eight years and his regime has produced a new China. China's turn outward to the West is certainly one of the significant events of the twentieth century!

(Editor's note: While this manuscript was being prepared for publication, Deng retired.)

Notes

1. *The Department of State Bulletin*, March 20, 1972, p. 433.

2. The *Courier Journal*, Louisville, Kent. Thursday, September 15, 1985, p. A6.

3. Edwin Munsel Bliss, *The Missionary Enterprise* (New York: Fleming H. Revell, 1908), p. 38.

4. Chen Zemin, vice principal, National Christian Seminary, Nanjing, China, as reported in *China Notes,* Winter 1984-1985, p. 320.

5. Frank Gibney in *Britannica Book of the Year* (Chicago: University of Chicago, 1980), pp. 9-11.

2

Prairie Fires and Mustard Seed

Guangzhou (Canton)

I walked into the People's Republic of China (PRC) on my first visit in July 1978!

A 5:15 wake-up call in the Hong Kong Hilton signaled "bags in the hall," coffee in the lobby, and a hurried departure for the Kowloon Railway Station. No U.S. tourists had visited China for twenty-seven years. Now the new leadership of the PRC was gingerly lifting the Bamboo Curtain.

The train was a "milk run" north through the Crown Colony's New Territories. Hong Kong's spectacular economic success was everywhere apparent, smoking industrial complexes, towering high-rises, a prosperous countryside of farmhouses, duck ponds, gardens, livestock, and TV antennae. At every stop the train platforms were jammed with people. Women in black pantaloons shouldering wicker baskets of vegetables pushed their way through the crowd. Suited businessmen and chic office workers in stylish dresses ran down the platform to find a car with empty seats. Shoppers loaded with transistor radios, TVs, and packages stood in the aisles. The atmosphere was electrifying. These people were happy, in a hurry, going somewhere!

One hour later the British train came to the end of the line at Lo Wu. I got off and walked with my baggage across a covered railroad bridge to the Chinese border checkpoint of Zhenzhen.

We passed through customs and immigration in a cavernous yellow brick hall. On the walls were billboard-size pictures of Mao flanked by red flags. Great banners with three-foot, bright red Chinese characters were draped across the hall. These were the sayings of Mao: "Be strong and fulfill the task of the Great New Period." "Build up the country through Socialist power." Hundred of copies of Mao's "little red book" (in English), the "Bible" of Chinese Communism, were stacked high on the concession counter.

A Glimpse of Old China

We boarded an ancient steam-powered train that would have quickened the pulse of any railroad buff! The vintage chair car reflected the luxury of a bygone day. The huge double seats swiveled to face a spacious bay window. The faded velour backs were covered with freshly starched handmade lace.

As soon as we got under way, a hostess dressed in drab blue pants and a white blouse came down the aisle carrying a battered aluminum teakettle. She filled our pint-sized, flowered China cups. For the next two hours, we sipped jasmine tea and watched the countryside of Old China unfold before us.

There were compounds of ancient stone and brick buildings with roofs of red tile and thatch. There were fields of sugarcane and rice, orchards of peach trees, bananas, papaya, and date palms. Aqueducts and pumping stations lifted water from canals into the rice paddies. Oxen grazed on the high banks of the checkerboard fields. Farmers rested at lunch under the eucalyptus trees. We saw an occasional truck, many "walking" tractors, three-wheeled tricycles, and unnumbered bicycles. Peasants, knee-deep in water, worked the rice paddies with lumbering water buffalo hitched to harrowlike wooden plows. Women balanced heavily loaded wicker baskets swung from shoulder poles. Men seined the fish ponds. Farmers threshed rice as their ancestors had done for centuries, with oxen treading the threshing floor.

All was plain and drab. Life moved slowly and mechanically. The panorama of Old China flashed before us like a slow-motion picture, a way of life unhurried and unchanged through the ages.

Time Is Money

Eight years and several China journeys later, in 1986, I entered China along the same train route. The changes were unbelievable!

We sped across the countryside in a new, luxurious, air-conditioned electric train. We stayed in the same seats on the same train all the way to Guangzhou, barely acknowledging the border crossing.

The sleepy little China border village of Zhenzhen with its rice paddies and fish ponds is no more! Instead, there is a modern city of three hundred thousand, with a greater concentration of high-rise buildings than can be found anywhere else in China, including Beijing and Shanghai. There are discotheques, private villas with swimming pools, duty-free consumer goods, and a prosperous citizenship. Here China is trying to create as quickly as possible its own model of prosperity and economic development under a special system that some Chinese solemnly call "state capitalism." Zhenzhen is an open city with one of fourteen special enterprise zones.

Gone are the solemn-faced pictures of Mao that hung in the immigration hall. Gone are the big character banners that carried his sayings. Instead, Zhenzhen has new slogans: "Time is money." "Efficiency is life." The government now exhorts the people to "create more material wealth for the state."

No Dogs, No Chinese

I spent my first night in China in Guangzhou's Dongfang Hotel, a sprawling concrete structure with threadbare carpets, worn-out mattresses, and antiquated plumbing. On my last visit I stayed in a new luxury hotel built on Shamian Island in the middle of the Pearl River.

Shamian Island was formerly a foreign concession, an exclusive enclave of banks, clubs, legations, and residences, posted with a notorious sign, "No dogs, no Chinese allowed." The new White Swan Hotel on the island has twenty-eight floors, one thousand rooms, thirty dining rooms, a staff of two thousand, and was built at a cost of fifty million dollars.

Many such luxury hotels are being built throughout China, joint ventures of the Chinese government and overseas capital. I went back to the Dongfang and found that it had been completely refurbished and the hotel lobby was banked with slot machines for the tourists.

There is a frequently told story of an old soldier, a veteran of China's civil war, who, seeing such changes, burst into tears and asked, "Is this what we fought the revolution for?" Certainly, this is not what Mao Zedong had in mind. For better or for worse, China has joined the twentieth-century world of the West.

"No Anchor Here"

Guangzhou is a steamy, subtropical city straddling the Pearl, China's fourth largest river. On my first visit we took an afternoon cruise up the river. It was alive with traffic, oceangoing vessels loaded with freight from Hong Kong, grain-laden barges tied in tow and pulled by a tug, boats piled high with brick and coal, with gunwales riding the surface and ferries jammed with passengers and bicycles.

I saw a steepled stone church on the south bank and asked Mr. Woo, our guide, about it. "Closed, of course. A warehouse, I think." He translated a large yellow and black triangular sign in front of the church for me. It said "No Anchor Here."

Stalled in traffic in a sea of bicycles as far as the eye could see, Mr. Woo woefully complained, "We have five million people and two million bicycles in Guangzhou." We were on our way to Yuexiu Park on Goat Hill where a statue of five goats commemorates the founding of Guangzhou. According to legend five celestial beings riding on goats, each bearing an ear of rice in its mouth, descended from heaven. They landed on this fertile bend in the Pearl River and established the city in 800 BC.

"Cantonese people love to eat," laughed Mr. Woo, pointing out the many restaurants in the downtown area. "Other Chinese say we eat anything with four legs except the kitchen table and anything with wings except an airplane." One Guangzhouese restaurant, The Dragon, features special dishes of dog and snake. Another claims a menu selection of over one thousand dishes.

Guangdong Province is the birthplace of Dr. Sun Yatsen. He is memorialized by a magnificent cylindrical templelike Assembly Hall, seating 4,500, constructed without pillars and providing every seat with an unobstructed view of the stage. Sun Yatsen studied to be a medical doctor. However, he became a revolutionary leader when he saw the desperate plight of the common people. In October 1911 the revolutionary armies took a provincial city in south China and, within a year, overthrew the centuries-old feudal imperial system. The Chinese Republic was established, and Dr. Sun Yatsen was made the first president.

"Dr. Sun Yatsen was the father of our country, our 'George Washington,'" Mr. Woo said, impressing us with his knowledge of American history.

No Christians Here

Later, in the restaurant atop the six-hundred-year-old peak-gabled Zenhai Tower built on the city's highest hill, we had a marvelous panoramic view of the broad bend in the Pearl River that circled Guangzhou. Sipping tea with Mr. Woo, I asked, "How did you know that we called George Washington the 'Father' of our country?"

"From the Americans in a Presbyterian mission school," he replied. "My father was a teacher."

"Was he a Christian?"

"Of course. He was of the old generation."

"And you? A Christian like your father?" asked my traveling companion, Duke McCall.

"I do not believe," he simply stated. And then, as if reflecting, he continued, "We have been taught 'There is no God.' I am not really an atheist. I just do not believe." His voice seemed to trail off into silent futility and he finished, "in anything."

Recalling the "No Anchor" church on the river, I asked, "Is there any church open in Guangzhou?"

"No," Mr. Woo said.

"Do you know any Christians?"

An anxious look clouded Mr. Woo's face. He seemed to be searching for a polite noncommittal way to end the conversation. He slowly shook his head, paused, and said, "It is time to go. We have much to see."

Rendezvous at Night

Back at the Dongfang Hotel I pondered Mr. Woo's response. What about his father? Was it a shadow of fear on his face? Had he, too, once been a believer? Was he a secret believer now?

I knew of one Christian in Guangzhou. His name and phone number had been given me in Hong Kong.

I found a phone booth in the hotel lobby and gave the number to the woman at the desk. On signal from the switchboard, I picked up the phone. It rang and there was an answer.

"Mr. Chen. Please, Mr. Chen." I said in the most articulate way I could. "Speak English? Mr. Chen, please."

The voice on the other end kept responding each time with the same monosyllabic word, which I assumed to be "what" or "who" or, maybe, "louder."

So I spoke louder. "Mr. Chen, please."

There was a flurry of Chinese, and then the voice said, "He not here."

So the person did know some English. Very slowly I told my name. I was a friend of Mr. Chen's brother in Hong Kong. I would like to meet Mr. Chen by the gate of the Dongfang Hotel tonight at eight o'clock. Please tell him. There was another long flurry of Chinese and silence. He hung up.

Shortly before eight I stood beside the stone-pillared gateway of the hotel compound. I carried a Chinese newspaper folded around a Bible commentary sent to Mr. Chen by his brother.

Presently an older man in a worn, unpressed Mao-style gray suit approached. Our eyes met in recognition. "Let us walk together slowly and we can talk," Chen said. "If we stand here, a crowd will gather."

Chen apologized for the telephone conversation. "Others were listening," he explained. A Hong Kong missionary later told me she heard by the Chinese grapevine that two "officials" came by to question Chen. "Why did a foreigner call you? Who was he? What did he want?"

Chen talked freely about being a Christian in China. He became a baptized believer in a Baptist church as a boy. After the missionaries left in 1949, the church remained open under Chinese leadership. He was a Sunday School teacher and lay leader in the church. Then came the Cultural Revolution. The young Red Guards closed and sacked the church.

"Then one day, they came to my house," he said. "They took all my books and burned them in the street. They sat me on a stool, put a dunce cap on my head, and shouted at me. They called me an 'enemy of the revolution' and spit on me. They beat me with sticks. I covered my face with my hands to protect my eyes. They quit only when I fell off the stool, unconscious."

Three months later, Chen was sent to a farm many miles northeast of Guangzhou. The hard work in the fields was "productive labor to reeducate him." He was separated from his family for six years. Finally he was allowed to return to the city.

"Yes, there are other Christians," he told me, "in private house churches." How many, he did not know, nor would he guess. Chen was the leader of one of these small groups. The Bible commentary would be a great help to him, he said.

"Is there still persecution?" I asked.

"No, the persecution has stopped." Chen continued, "Yes, the situation is much better. The 'Gang of Four' is in prison. The house churches are meeting more frequently, but still secretly. We must be very careful."

We were back at the gates of the hotel, and Chen faded into the darkness. I wondered how many others there were in China like him, unnamed and known only to God, still faithful through years of suffering.

A Great Work of the Spirit

Two years later I was again in Guangzhou, in the summer of 1980, again at the Dongfang Hotel. My wife, Lealice, and I were in the taxi lot very close to the stone gatepost where I had met Mr. Chen on that memorable summer night in 1978. We loaded a box of books into a taxi and gave the driver an address written in Chinese, No. 9 Jian Tong Jin.

It seemed about two miles to Guangzhou's eastern suburbs when we came to a magnificent towered stone church with a sign, Dong Shan Church (which means "Eastern Hills" in Chinese). We passed through the green wrought iron gates, through the courtyard and into a spacious sanctuary that would seat 1,800.

Church leaders were waiting to greet us. Mr. Do (a layman and Baptist deacon), Kao Young Chung (a British Methodist layman), the Reverend Harold Wong (pastor of the Zion Church), the Reverend Fan Sheu

Yean (one of the four pastors of the Dong Shan Church); Ms. Mak Wai San (a Baptist church worker), and others.

We were ushered into a side room for tea. As I laid out the commentaries, devotional books, Bibles, hymnbooks, and church manuals from Hong Kong, I said, "Tell us, what is happening here?"

"Oh," Pastor Fan replied as his face beamed and his eyes sparkled, "there is a great work of the Spirit of God taking place here." His excitement was galvanic! The church, like all others in China, had been closed during the Cultural Revolution and used as a community hall. Then, under a new government policy, the property was returned to the church and reopened on September 30, 1979.

"The church was packed with over two thousand people," he continued. "Now we must put paper on the floor, the aisles, and the steps for people to sit on. Forty percent of those who attend are young people, along with many professionals and intellectuals, doctors, teachers, engineers."

"Other churches are opening, too," the Reverend Harold Wong told us. "The Zion Church, where I am pastor in the central city near the Dongfang Hotel, is being renovated. We expect to open in two months. The South Pearl River Church will open the first of the year."

"How many churches are open in China?" I asked.

"It is happening so fast," Mr. Do, the deacon and secretary for the Guangzhou churches, replied. "Some say 'a church a week' is opening. Others say 'a church a day,' all over China."

A United Church

"All Protestants are united in one church," Pastor Fan said. "Here at Dong Shan we have Baptist, Methodists, Anglicans, Lutherans, Seventh-Day Adventists. We are all 'one in Christ.'"

"Our greatest need is leadership," Pastor Fan said. "Our senior pastor, the Reverend Matthew Tong, is seventy-three." (I learned that a short time later Pastor Tong died.)

Fan continued, "Throughout China, it is the same. The trained pastors are very old. For thirty years there have been no young people preparing for the ministry. But a seminary will open in Nanjing this fall. We already have fifteen young people from our church ready to go. But the seminary can take only forty students and there will be hundreds of applications from all over China. Churches are opening, but leadership for the churches is a major problem."

"Do you need Bibles?" I asked.

"We are publishing fifty-five thousand Bibles, and eighty thousand New Testaments in Shanghai. Our church sent thirty thousand yuan (about ten thousand dollars) for the project. The Bibles will sell for five yuan, New Testaments for two yuan."

The Three-Self Movement

Mr. Kao Young Chung is general secretary of the Three-Self Committee for Guangzhou. We talked at length about the Three-Self Patriotic Movement.

In May of 1950 (the year after the Communist revolution) nineteen Christian leaders, representing all Protestant denominations, formed an emergency committee. The committee was led by three influential Christians, the national secretary of the YMCA, Dr. Y. T. Wu, along with Ai Nien-San, a prominent Lutheran, and a Methodist bishop, Z. T. Kaung. The purpose of the committee was to assess the problems the churches faced and to appeal to the new government to protect the constitutional rights of Chinese Christians to worship freely.

First, Christians faced a new political situation. A philosophically atheistic regime was in power.

Second, the missionaries were gone. Churches and institutions were weakened. Foreign financial support had been cut off. Protestant Christianity was splintered into rival denominations and floundering for direction.

Third, there was a public mistrust and hatred of all things foreign. Rightly or wrongly, Christianity was perceived as a foreign religion imposed upon the Chinese by the Western imperialists. There was a saying, "Every time a Chinese becomes a Christian, the Church gains a member and China loses a citizen."

Finally, soldiers and local officials were harassing and persecuting

Christian citizens in spite of the initial promise of the new government to allow freedom of religion.

The committee met with Premier Zhou Enlai at nine o'clock one night. The meeting, scheduled for two hours, lasted all night. The committee asked for an "official guarantee" of religious freedom and a cessation of persecution.

Zhou admitted there had been violations at the local level. But he was adamant. "You must cut the imperialist ties." There were vigorous and heated discussions. By morning, the committee had hammered out a proposal for a church that would be all Chinese, patriotic, and free from all foreign influence. The formula was simple: "Self-Government, Self-Support, Self-Propagation"—the "Three-Self Patriotic Church."

Atheism's Gauntlet

Zhou Enlai accepted the Three-Self concept and pledged that the government would make an honest effort to check all violations of religious freedom, to protect the rights of all citizens, and to ensure Three-Self churches the freedom to function.

Then Zhou threw down the gauntlet. "We are going to let you go on teaching, go on trying to convert the people. . . . We both know that truth will prevail. We think your beliefs are untrue and false . . . therefore if we are right, the people will reject them . . . if you are right then the people will believe you . . . we are prepared to take that risk."[1]

Zhou obviously saw in the Three-Self Church nothing more than a movement to mobilize the resources of Chinese Christians in an anti-imperialist campaign. He and the Communists failed to calculate that the inevitable direction of any gathering of Christians under any slogan or title would eventually lead to the ultimate objects of the salvation of souls and the spiritual upbuilding of the church. Selfhood and an indigenous Chinese church are in the providence of God, even though they had to come through the trauma of war and persecution. Chinese Christianity needed weaning from mission support, and the churches needed to be dewesternized.

Selfhood was the vision of the missionary thrust in China from the beginning. Robert Morrison, the first Protestant missionary who went to

China in 1807, envisioned an independent Chinese church and declared, "The final triumphs of the Gospel will be by means of native missionaries and the Bible." Later, in the 1800s, Henry Venn, Secretary of the Church Missionary Society in London, and Rufus Anderson, Secretary of the American Board of Commissioners in Boston, articulated the three-self formula as the ultimate missionary objective. Dr. Visser T'Hooft, General Secretary of the World Council of Churches in the 1950s reemphasized missions as culminating in self-supporting, self-determining and self-propagating national churches. Dr. J. R. Mott, who sparked the Student Volunteer Movement for Foreign Missions, defined the task of missionaries: to "develop indigenous churches" that would make the "missionaries dispensable."

The End of the Missionary Era

After the meeting with Zhou, the committee took their Three-Self agreement to the people. In July 1950 a document known as the Christian Manifesto was signed by the forty committee leaders and was circulated through the churches in China. Within two years it received over four hundred thousand signatures. Half the total Protestant membership of China had signed it. The manifesto set forth a singularly clear policy and program. The churches of China were to use no foreign funds and no foreign personnel. Education, medical, and charitable institutions were to be turned over to the government. At that time the government did not take over the theological seminaries and Bible schools but left them to the direction of churches. The churches also retained the Bible houses and other Chinese publishing companies.

The government did not officially expel foreign missionaries from China. There was intense pressure and harassment. Missionaries were told to be nonparticipants and not to be involved in church or educational activities.

When the United Nations intervened in Korea in 1950, increased pressure was exerted upon foreign missionaries still remaining in China (especially Americans). They were looked upon with great suspicion and mistrust and suspected of counterrevolutionary or reactionary activity. Thousands of other Chinese people besides Christians were arrested, imprisoned, and executed in public demonstrations as a part of the "three-anti" campaign (antiwaste, anticorruption, antibureaucracy). This was a desperate and violent attempt on the part of the new government to purge society of these evils.

In January 1951 the largest and longest established mission, the China Inland Mission, gave orders for the complete evacuation of all missionaries, 601 adults and 284 children. Others followed. By 1952 what had existed of foreign missionary involvement in China for 140 years was completely eliminated. All universities that had been founded and maintained on foreign Christian initiative had either been forcibly merged or had disappeared. The modern missionary era in China had ended.[2]

In the late fifties and early sixties, the small Protestant movement, the Three-Self churches, struggled to take root in Chinese soil. Then came the devastating Cultural Revolution. All churches were closed, confiscated, looted, sacked, or burned by the rampaging young radicals of the Red Guard. Church leaders and members alike suffered. Mao and Zhou both died, the Gang of Four was ousted, and the new regime under Deng Xiaoping took the helm in 1976.

By 1980 the winds of change in the new China began to bring fresh hope to the beleaguered and suffering Christian remnant. Along with the liberalization of government policy in economics, education, and the arts, there was a call for this liberalization to be extended to religion.

A New Manifesto

In March 1980 the standing committee of the national Three-Self Movement met in Shanghai. It was their first meeting in ten years! Out of that meeting came a two-thousand-word open letter circulated in China and to the churches in the West. It was hailed by many as "the most important religious document to emerge from China since 1949."[3]

In summary the open letter said that in the recent past "the policy of religious freedom has been trespassed upon" (referring to the Cultural Revolution). It called upon the Chinese government to restore full religious liberty according to the pact of the Three-Self Committee of 1950 and the guarantees of the Chinese constitution. It called upon foreign churches abroad to recognize this "right of selfhood and freedom for the

Chinese churches" and not to violate this cherished principle of selfhood in the name of evangelism.

It further declared that Chinese Christianity could not be pushed back into the colonial past. This was a direct response to those who asked, "When can we send missionaries back into China?"

The Mustard Seed

That night in the Dong Shan Three-Self Church of Guangzhou we talked and drank tea until after midnight.

"A Three-Self Church, self-control, self-support, self-propagation. That sounds like a Baptist church to me." I winked and nodded at the Baptist deacon, Mr. Do.

"Not so," Mr. Kao, the British Methodist layman, fired back. "Sounds more like a New Testament church to me." He grinned, knowing he was one up.

Finally we joined hands in a circle of prayer, sang "Blest be the tie that binds Our hearts in Christian love," and went out into the night.

"I feel tonight that we have reached back through twenty centuries and captured something of the spirit of that first church gathered with the Lord at the Last Supper," I said to Lealice as we rode back to the hotel.

As we came out of the Eastern Hills, the lights of Guangzhou's center city came into view. There were the landmarks, the Kwanto Hotel, the Sun Yatsen Memorial, and, to the left, the tall government building on the site of the original National Peasant Movement Institute where the revolution was born. On top of the building was the giant, ever-burning red torch.

I remembered what our guide, Mr. Woo, had said two years before. "That is a memorial to Chairman Mao. Mao said, 'A single spark can start a prairie fire.' That is a symbol of the revolution!"

Symbols!

A flaming torch . . . the light of the world.

A fiery spark . . . body broken, blood shed.

A prairie fire consuming all . . . a mustard seed growing into a
mighty tree where all life can find refuge.

Notes

1. Victor E. W. Haywood, *Christians and China* (Belfast: Christian Journals, Limited, 1974), p. 55.

2. For a fuller treatment of this era see C. Jones, *The Church in Communist China: A Protestant Appraisal* (N.Y.: Friendship Press, 1962).

3. Jim Castelli, "Church Partly Free in China," *The Washington Star* June 14, 1980.

3

The Seed of the Church
Guilin (Kweilin)

"The river forms a green silk belt, the mountains are like blue jade hairpins." Thus Han Yu, the celebrated T'ang Dynasty poet of 1,200 years ago described the area around Guilin, a city in the Guangxi region of southwest China. To this day it is considered the most beautiful countryside in all China. The image that most Westerners have of the landscape of China is actually that of Guilin. Through the centuries Chinese artists have painted the mist-shrouded mountains and immortalized the scenery.

On the Li

We seemed to be floating in a misty ethereal dreamland. Only the vibrating grind of the engine kept us in touch with reality as our sightseeing boat groaned and lurched against the crystalline river currents. As we maneuvered through twisting channels and dodged broad bending shoals, the swish on the hull and the rippling song of the shallows played a symphony to the visual drama of sunlight and shadow on the mirrored waters. Cliffs, crags, and gigantic fingerlike mountains a thousand feet high reflected in ever-changing hues and colors, and, softened by patches of cloudy mist, painted a living scroll of traditional Chinese art before our eyes.

As hundreds of thousands of other tourists have done, we brought our grueling China tour to a climax with this final totally relaxing, idyllic experience, a cruise on China's famous Li River.

The river was alive with activity. Children splashed in the shallows while water buffalo waded belly-deep on the flats and ducked their heads under water to graze off the aquatic plants on the bottom. Farmers worked the fields with shovel-bladed hoes while women scurried about in the yards of the mud brick farmhouses. Straining ferrymen poled long boats loaded with people, baskets, and bicycles across the river.

As we cruised along, our guide pointed out the sights. We stretched our imagination and compromised the truth by affirming that we saw clearly what he so plainly pointed out. There was Elephant Trunk Hill, "obviously an elephant drinking from the river," and Old Man Mountain, "unmistakably the head and neck of a man" in profile. But Nine Horse Hill, a series of chalk cliffs in the bend of the river, confounded us. Our guide pointed out the knobs and hills that resembled nine horses in different poses, one neighing, another bending to drink, a third lying down. At the same time, another guide just aft of us was telling her group that the name, Nine Horse Hill, came from nine petroglyphs of horses carved by primitive men. If you looked where she pointed, she said, you could distinctly see them on the face of the cliffs.

At the end of the cruise, we disembarked at the fishing village of Yangshou. From there we took a bus back to Guilin through the "finger" mountains, gigantic thousand-foot battlements, and conical peaks of limestone scattered like trees across the countryside. These geological structures are found in only one other place in the world, in Yugoslavia. The karst formations were thrust up from the limestone bed of a sea which once covered the region. The erosion of wind and water over the millenia carved out this haunting otherworldly landscape.

The Cinnamon Forest

Guilin means "Cassia woods." Cassia, or cinnamon trees, canopy the city's streets and are indigenous to the area. Today Guilin is primarily a tourist town, not unlike many Western resort areas. Pedicabs solicit tourists at the entrance to the hotel. Street vendors crowd visitors, hawking hats, postcards, and slides, bargaining and tugging sleeves. Handcraft and food stalls line the downtown sidewalks. Antique and souvenir shops are everywhere.

Guilin has not always been this open to visitors, nor the countryside as tranquil and idyllic. The city is in the upper part of the vast Hsi

Chiang (West River) basin that empties into the South China Sea at the Portuguese port of Macao (just forty miles west of Hong Kong). The region has been occupied by the non-Chinese Zhuang people from classical antiquity. They are a part of the indigenous Tai language group of Southeast Asia. The Zhuang have readily absorbed Chinese culture and language but are principally Muslim in religion. In the mountains are three smaller minorities, the Yao, Miao, and T'ung.

The twelve million Zhuang are China's largest minority group and 90 percent of them live in the Guangxi Zhuang Autonomous Region. There are five such autonomous regions in China, distinct from the twenty-one provinces (similar to our states) and three municipalities (Beijing, Shanghai, and Tianjin, which are similar to our District of Columbia). The autonomous regions have a special political status and are designated homelands for fifty-five minority groups of China.

Guangxi is on the periphery of China, adjoining Vietnam to the southwest and directly above the Gulf of Tonkin. During the empire era, interior areas of the region were never completely subdued but were controlled by a system of indirect rule through chieftains and minor warlords. This continued until the middle of this century. Over the years there have been continuous troubles and major uprisings in the region. River pirates controlled the remote river passages, and bandit gangs harassed the isolated hill country.

The Arrival of the Gospel

Downstream from Guilin on the West River, 150 miles as the crow flies, is Wuzhou. This river port city is accessible to oceangoing vessels up to one thousand tons and is the water gateway to the Zhuang Region.

In 1862 the first Baptist missionary, R. H. Graves, came up the river to Wuzhou from Guangdong (then Kwangtung). He wrote in his diary, "The natives of the province were strongly opposed to a foreigner settling in their midst and met every attempt at entrance with a determined opposition which reached the point of mob violence and bloodshed."[1] Because of the hostility of the residents, Graves could go ashore only during the day to do his evangelistic work and had to return to his ship each night.

When the British forced an open trade treaty on Beijing in 1897, Wuzhou was one of the cities designated as a treaty port. Commerce flowed freely up the river from Macao and Hong Kong. Missionaries poured into Guangxi Province: the Christian Missionary Alliance, the Baptists, the Anglicans, the Lutherans, the Methodists, the Pentecostal Holiness, the Seventh-day Adventists, the Little Flock, the Gospel Boat. Spreading from the base in Wuzhou, mission centers were established in the other principal cities of the province, Guilin, Liuzhou, and Nanning.

In Wuzhou, Baptists and Methodists both developed a strong medical and educational work. The Baptists built Stout Memorial Hospital, a five-story facility on a beautiful hillside on the outskirts of Wuzhou overlooking the West River. In 1935 a tall, lanky missionary doctor from the hills of Tennessee, William L. Wallace, came to Wuzhou to be the hospital surgeon. Fifteen years later, the name of Dr. Bill Wallace would be written on the immortal pages of Christian martyrs. I tell his story because it gives an insight into what happened to many Western missionaries and Chinese Christians throughout the country in those final chaotic days when the Nationalist government fell and the Communist regime took over.

The Beginning of the End

In the early part of the 1949 the Nationalist troops were in retreat. Then Beijing was taken. On October 1, Mao proclaimed the People's Republic as the new government of China. Mop-up military operations continued throughout China.

Later in the month of October the Nationalists abandoned Guilin. The Communist troops took over and continued down the West River. Missionaries of all denominations poured into Wuzhou from the interior of Southwest China. Most continued on to safety in Hong Kong and Macao. Wuzhou was the only Baptist mission station in China not in the hands of the Communists.

Several mission boards evacuated all missionaries. Southern Baptists left the decision with individual missionaries.

"I am a doctor," Bill Wallace said. "I help people. Whatever happens politically, sick people will need medical care. I will stay as long as I can do any good." Bill was advised that the United States did not recognize the new regime, and he would not have the protection of an American consulate in case of trouble. "My work is humanitarian. I will not be in danger. Besides, I am here serving Christ" was his answer.

A month later, on Thanksgiving Day, 1949, Communist troops marched down the streets of Wuzhou. Thousands paraded with them, shouting, clashing cymbals, and carrying signs, "China for the Chinese."

The events that followed in Wuzhou occurred all over China in varying degrees of intensity. The violence was more severe in Guangxi perhaps because of the remoteness of the province from the authority of a central government and also because of a long history of resistance to all foreigners. First came the "accusation meetings." These were giant people's courts for everyone suspected of being counterrevolutionary. There were massive arrests.[2]

In Wuzhou, first the landlords were rounded up. They were paraded through the streets, bound and wearing dunce caps and slanderous placards. They were abused and beaten; then the public trials began. The crowds shouted the accusations, rendered the verdict, and passed the judgment. Some were sentenced to immediate death; others, to prison; others, to prison farms for years of hard labor and reeducation.

Every week the accusation meetings continued. More people were ferreted out and arrested for "antirevolutionary activities" or "foreign imperialistic leanings." At that time the persecution of the Christians by the ultraleftists began. Christians were called "demons and monsters" and "imperialistic traitors." These were dark days. Few, if any, Christians in all Guangxi escaped suffering for their choice of belief in a foreign religion. Some died for their beliefs.[3]

Dr. Wallace and the hospital staff continued to function, ministering to all who needed medical aid (including Communist soldiers). But they were continually harassed by unreasonable regulations, false charges, and bitter threats. The real crisis came in the next year, June 1950, when the Korean War began. "Hate America" rallies were staged and scathing denunciations were leveled against the "Yankee dogs" and the "imperialistic wolves."

When China entered the Korean War in December on the side of the North Koreans, China was, for all practical purposes, at war with America. Throughout China, the purge of all things foreign and American began in earnest.

Arrested

At 3 AM there was a knock on the door of Bill Wallace's apartment. "Open up, we have a sick man here," a voice pleaded in the dark. As he opened the door, a dozen young soldiers barged in. "You are under arrest as President Truman's chief spy in south China. We know your hospital is a den of spies."

With Bill Wallace's arrest, the Baptist Mission property, Stout Memorial Hospital, was taken over and renamed The Workers Hospital. It continues in operation today under this name.

The arrest of the missionary doctor and the expropriation of the property in Wuzhou was not an isolated incident. All over China, within a matter of weeks, $41,900,000 worth of foreign mission properties were either expropriated or closed. The twelve Protestant Christian colleges run by the United Board for the Christian Colleges in China were taken over (including the prestigious Baptist Shanghai University). The Beijing Union Medical College and Changsha's "Yale in China" were expropriated. The Catholics lost 506 hospitals, 905 dispensaries, 31 leprosariums, 320 orphanages, and more than 6,000 schools.[4]

The American missionaries were not the sole targets of the ultraleftist fury. All over China, thousands of Chinese Christian leaders were also arrested. One pastor interpreted to me what happened.

"The Korean War created a climate in China that caused great suffering for all Christians. The war mobilized the Chinese people against the West. Citizens were asked to give part of their salary to buy airplanes, bombs, and bullets. Many of us (pastors, professors, students) were pacifists and refused to contribute to the war effort." For this, he was arrested as an American imperialist sympathizer and convicted.

"They first sent me away for six months to study Marxism, 'to get my thinking straight.' It was the 'three-eight' system, eight hours of physical labor, eight hours of political study, eight hours of rest." Most of the others at the 'reeducation school' were professors, not pastors or religious persons.

"I remember as I was telling my wife good-bye, I prayed, *I know you are a living God, but God, please don't blow out all the candles just to show me how dark it is.* That prayer has been ringing in my heart now for thirty-five years. I had to give up my church and my preaching. I was sent to teach hundreds of miles from my home. I was never allowed to move back with my wife and family, and they were never allowed to move to be with me."[5]

To Live Is Christ

In Wuzhou many other foreigners, including a Catholic nun, several priests, and a bishop, were arrested along with Dr. Bill Wallace. The imprisonment of the forty-year-old missionary doctor lasted fifty-three days. Bill Wallace was very popular with many influential local people. During fifteen years of sacrificial humane service, he had made many friends. There was considerable public discontent with his arrest. The new ultraleftist regime sought desperately to discredit him and force a confession from him.

In the weeks that followed his arrest, Bill Wallace was paraded through the streets with an obscene placard hung around his neck. He was beaten and abused. He was shouted at and harassed. He was accused of "incompetence in surgery," "murdering and maiming Chinese patients," "performing illegal and obscene operations." For four weeks they sought to break him down, to brainwash him thoroughly, and to get a confession from him. On his fifty-third night in prison, guards came to his cell, according to the testimony of two priests who were cellmates. The guards carried long bamboo poles. They thrust them between the bars to jab and harass the sleeping American doctor. In their zeal to torment him, they must have miscalculated. Or their actions may have been deliberate. They cruelly pounded him to death with the butt end of the poles. The next morning the guards simply announced publicly that Bill Wallace had hanged himself.

That day Bill Wallace was buried in a cheap wooden coffin in a bamboo-shaded cemetery on a hill overlooking the West River. The soldiers would not allow a service to be held. When the grave was filled, they drove the crowd away. Later Chinese friends collected money and built a cement terrace on the grave and erected a single shaft reaching heavenward. On the shaft they inscribed in simple Scripture their estimate of the life of Bill Wallace: "For to Me to Live is Christ."[6]

The Guilin Church

Throughout the Guangxi region, the ranks of open believers were decimated by these early persecutions. In 1949 in the provincial capital of Guilin were four Protestant churches: Baptist, Congregational, Anglican, and Presbyterian. But as this wave of persecutions took its toll, attendance dwindled. Finally all churches were combined into one, meeting in the Baptist property in downtown Guilin. In 1960 that church was closed by the Red Guards of the Cultural Revolution, and the building was converted to "productive use for the benefit of the people" as a printing house and book bindery.

Within the last few years, the frightened and timid believers in Guangxi, long remembering the more than twenty-five bitter years of suffering, have begun to emerge from their secret meetings and cautiously express their faith. Churches are beginning to open up again.

In Guilin on a summery Monday night in 1986 at 8:30 PM, a pedicab dropped me off in front of the blackened stone church with broken windows on the second floor and a small metal cross at the top of the facade. I walked down the alley beside the church and knocked on the door at the rear of the compound. A petite, saintly looking elderly woman with snowy white hair, Ms. Ching, opened the door and in precise English greeted me. In the courtyard, laundry hung on the line. A wheelbarrow, buckets, sand, and lumber were piled to the side. Pots of flowers and greenery were set in the corners. Ms. Ching lived here with another woman and served as caretaker.

"I know Ms. Millie Lovegren" (a former China missionary now living in Oregon). "She has visited us five times already and is expected back again next month. I was in the church here with her before 1949," she said as we walked across the courtyard. Yes, she remembered the other missionaries who were there before the 1949 revolution: the Lawtons, the Creeks, and the Merrits.

We stepped into the sanctuary with its slatted benches, dingy walls, a piano to the side, a pulpit on the rostrum.

"We are making repairs now," she said. "The attendance is increasing every week. Many young people are coming."

She told me the church now has a membership of 200 and conducts a hymn sing on Friday nights, a prayer service on Wednesday nights, and a Sunday service from 1:00 to 2:30 PM.

I had come to attend the deacons' meeting. Ms. Ching explained that she, too, was a deacon and had been sent to the gate to wait for me. She led me into a small meeting room that served as the church office. In the center was a simple wooden table and on it a few scattered papers, an inkwell and pen, two gray hardback record books, and a green-shaded metal lamp.

I met the pastor, Lou Yu-feng, a tall, lean, sharp-faced, angular man who spoke no English. He had been a Seventh-Day Adventist. Mr. Yen, a teacher of Chinese and English at the Guilin Normal School, was to be my translator. There was another deacon, a retired factory worker who was head of the local Three-Self Committee, and a second woman deacon. After a formal welcome they asked me to lead in prayer and then proceeded with the business of the church as Mr. Yen translated.

The agenda was no different than that I had followed in hundreds of deacons' meetings during forty-five years as a pastor. The concerns were universal: finances, renovation of the building, a report to be sent to the Three-Self headquarters in Nanjing, a national conference in Beijing, concerns for world peace, the examination of student applicants for admission to the new seminary opening in Guangzhou in the fall. The pastor emphasized that the mission of the church was spiritual. He discussed plans for an indoctrination class and a baptizing. The meeting closed as we joined hands in a circle of prayer.

Other churches have opened in Guangxi. In Liuzhou (to the east between Guilin and Wuzhou) a church has combined evangelism and social ministry in a remarkably successful way. The Liuzhou church manages a clothing processing factory in a workshop on the property. The factory has ninety-four family sewing machines, some donated by church members, in addition to nineteen industrial machines. Through this project the church receives income, contributes to the economy of the community, and provides job opportunities for young people and others without permanent jobs. The church has eight meeting points throughout the city where preaching services are conducted every week.

With only two pastors, the Liuzhou church relies heavily on lay leadership to operate the meeting points and the weekly Bible studies. Six services, stretched over three days, were required last Christmas to accommodate the crowds. Still, every service was packed, and people were in the courtyard and out to the gate trying to get in.

"Guangxi, at latest estimate, has over twelve thousand Christians, according to the Three-Self report," Mr. Yen told me.

"But we have only fifteen ordained pastors to serve the whole region," Pastor Luo said. "We have a desperate need for trained leadership. It is so easy for new believers to be led astray."

Recently, in the Liuzhou area, a self-appointed evangelist, Brother Fang, went through the countryside selling crosses made from red cloth that he claimed were charms against evil spirits. One peasant family bought seventeen. Claiming also to be an ordained elder, he baptized more than 180 people. He worshiped in no particular church. Wandering around, he asked "his believers" to donate to him money, chickens, ducklings, and other domestic animals.

Brother Fang's activities were declared illegal and superstitious by the local authorities. Although he was not jailed or fined, he was compelled to cease activity. Unfortunately formal public Christian activity was discredited by his deviations and was prohibited in the area for a while afterward.[7]

There was an outbreak of illegal activity by the Yellers and Shouters sects in another province near Shanghai. The Shouters created many problems in the prerevolutionary churches before 1949. The practice is beginning to take root again in some sections of China. These people disrupt church services by standing up and shouting, "Jesus is great, but I am greater."

"Disturbing worship is not only illegal but what the shouters say is heresy," a pastor explained. This errant doctrine appears to be based on the New Testament references where Jesus promised His followers that they would do even greater works than He did.

The Chinese do not look with favor on speaking in tongues, faith-healers, exorcism, magic, or fortune telling. The village shaman engaged in such practices and exploited the superstitions of the people in the past. Unlike in our country, where such aberrations are subject only to the control of public acceptance or rejection, China has laws that specifically forbid these practices.

The Chinese Christians do not sidestep the issue of divine healing. They pray to God for miracles of healing to be performed and believe that many times God does heal in a miraculous and supernatural way. A Guangxi pastor, the Reverend Shen Mingsul, said, "Actually, any Christian can pray directly to God and so communicate with God himself or herself without the need of a human 'healer.'"[8] A distinction is made between a *healing* and a *healer* who exploits the people by collecting fees for his "divine services."

A Private Mission

On May 7, 1982, Vice-President George Bush arrived in Beijing for an official diplomatic mission on behalf of the new Reagan administration. The agenda covered a long list of items—arms sales, trade, cultural exchanges, and the all-important "Taiwan Issue."

In a joint communique issued on August 17, both sides said that agreement had been reached on all matters and that the Reagan administration acceded to the Chinese proposition that the "People's Republic is the sole legal government of China."

There was also a private matter on Mr. Bush's agenda. He carried a letter containing a humanitarian request that the Chinese government release the remains of Dr. William Wallace for burial in the family cemetery in East Tennessee.

Beijing readily agreed, but there was no record anywhere of a Dr. Wallace or of an accused American spy being executed in Wuzhow by the Communist troops. Beijing sent instructions to Wuzhou, "Find this doctor's bones and release them."

The authorities in Wuzhou had problems. A grapevine report had come out of China fifteen years earlier that Bill Wallace's grave had been desecrated and destroyed. That was partially correct. In fact, the whole cemetery had been destroyed by a new road that was cut directly through it. Before road construction began, all residents in Wuzhou who had relatives buried in the cemetery were notified to move the graves.

Further investigation revealed that Christian friends took it upon themselves to dig up Bill Wallace's bones and rebury them in a private family plot. The officials exhumed his remains, placed them in a funerary jar, and stored them on the shelf in a Chinese funeral parlor, awaiting further instructions from Beijing. No one ever came for the bones.

Two years later a letter from Wuzhow was delivered to Ms. Cornelia Leavell, a retired missionary in Hong Kong. It said, "We have the bones of Dr. Bill Wallace. Send someone to get them."

Wuzhou was not yet open to tourists. Beijing's official policy of religious freedom and reopening churches had not yet penetrated this area. Christians were still afraid of discrimination and retaliation. All religious activity was still very secret and private. Cornelia recognized the letter as authentic, from a longtime friend in Wuzhou. A few months later Cornelia and a small group from Hong Kong took the 220-mile trip up the West River to Wuzhou to claim the remains of Dr. Wallace.[9]

Home at Last

Missionary martyr Dr. William L. Wallace's body came home at last to the hills of Tennessee to be reinterred with his family's ancestors. In the memorial service in Knoxville, the epitaph on the Wuzhou marker, "For to Me to Live is Christ," was completed: "And to Die is Gain" (Phil. 1:21).

Within the last year, Wuzhou has become an open tourist city. A high-speed hovercraft ferry carries thousands of visitors up the river.

A church now meets in the former Christian Missionary Alliance building. In the first Christmas service, the auditorium was packed. The service began in darkness with each member being given a candle. With the lighting of each small flame, the darkness retreated until suddenly the whole congregation was bathed in the light of the candles. Christ, the light of the world! Then carols were sung and the old and young mounted the platform to proclaim the good news of the birth of Jesus. All the darkness of the bitter years of suffering and death could not put out the light of the gospel.[10]

Notes

1. R. H. Graves in "The Church in Guangxi: Challenge to the Faithful," *The Bridge,* January-February 1985, 9:5-6.

2. As the ultra leftists came into power in October 1949, there were country-wide programs of "brainwashing," "thought reform" and "reeducation" of counterrevolutionaries. The total number arrested and tried in the public "accusation meetings" is unknown; 16,000 were arrested in one week in Shanghai alone.

3. *The Bridge,* 9:6.

4. *Time* magazine, January 8, 1951.

5. Since my first interview with this pastor who cautioned that I not put his name in print, I have visited with him again. He is convinced that the reforms are genuine and permanent and that there will not be a return to the religious persecution of the past. He said, "It is greatly changed now. The lights are on again in my life. The living God is with me. The church where I was pastor in another city has reopened. It is proclaiming the gospel again with another pastor. It is alive today because it is the living body of Christ."

6. Jesse C. Fletcher, *Bill Wallace of China* (Nashville: Broadman Press, 1963), pp. 141-151.

7. *The Bridge,* 9:7.

8. Shen Mingsul, ibid. p. 12.

9. Details of the recovery of Bill Wallace's remains were told to me by one of the participants in making the arrangements, the Reverend Gerald Hale in Hong Kong. He said, "The story of Bill Wallace influenced my call to missions more than anything else."

10. *The Bridge,* 9:8.

4

Finding a Lost God

Kunming

House churches were the survival cells of Christianity in China during the years when suspected Christians suffered untold persecutions, imprisonment, and death. The house church is not a unique Chinese innovation to Christianity. First-century Christians worshiped in their homes. Public church buildings were not constructed until the third century after Christ.[1] However, the house churches did produce a truly indigenous Chinese Christianity and freed China from dependence on foreign mission societies, funds, and personnel.

House churches had their beginnings during Mao's campaigns against all things foreign after he gained power in 1949. Protestant Christians began to worship in the privacy of their homes, and many Catholics joined them. They often gathered at night for prayer, studying of the Bible, and singing. They were led almost exclusively by laity, both male and female.

During the ten catastrophic years of the Cultural Revolution when all the churches were closed, the house churches kept functioning. They often met in such secrecy that it appeared Christianity had been eradicated in China. But the "silent ones" kept meeting, praying, witnessing, and studying in little family and close-knit neighborhood groups. Finally secret Christians began to emerge from their catacomb existence after 1978 and became the mainstream of Chinese Protestant Christianity. My first contact with a house church came early in my visits to China. It was in Kunming.

City of Eternal Spring

Kunming is a provincial capital in an isolated and remote section of southwest China bordering Vietnam, Laos, Burma, and western India. Marco Polo, the young Venetian adventurer, on his epochal journey to China seven centuries ago, visited Kunming. Then it was called Yunnanfu (from which is derived Yunnan, the name of the province today).

The city lies in an amphitheater of mountains on a high, fertile alluvial plain. To the south are the treacherous mountain jungles of North Vietnam; to the west, the mighty mountains of Burma and sky-high peaks of Tibet. An "Oriental Denver," Kunming is a mile-high city. But unlike its Rocky Mountain counterpart, Kunming is semitropical, one hundred miles north of the Tropic of Cancer at about the same southern latitude as steamy Calcutta. With cool summers and mild winters, it is a veritable year-round paradise, called by the Chinese "The City of Eternal Spring."

We went to Kunming in early summer. It was incredibly beautiful—golden with wheat, emblazoned with brilliant flowers, and abundant with semitropical fruits. The city lies on the northern shores of twenty-five-mile-long Lake Tien (Lake of Heaven). After 1949 the New Regime, consistent with its atheistic philosophy, changed the name to Dian Chi, The Shimmering Lake. Today it is more often called Lake Kunming.

A Glimpse of Yesterday

Kunming has a population of one million people and an expanding base of commerce and industry. Cut off by mountain ranges, and 1,250 miles from Beijing, Shanghai, and the cosmopolitan eastern coast, the city is considered by most Chinese to be the boondocks.

A walk through the twisted lanes and narrow streets of old Kunming is like turning back the pages of time to a fascinating yesterday in Old China. A grandmother sits on the steps of a red brick house patiently stuffing long slippery noodles with chopsticks, one by one, into the mouth of a baby. A Mongolian pony pulls a two-wheeled cart piled high with hay through the crowded alley. A scribe, at a street-side table, writes a letter dictated by an illiterate countryman. An enterprising youngster in a green army jacket peddles peanuts.

Our compassion was stirred by the sight of a farmer pushing a primitive wooden wheelbarrow. On it a woman sprawled limply, facedown and groaning, on her way to the clinic. Our compassion was stirred in a different way by the sight of another farmer pushing a wheelbarrow with a huge pig stretched across the bed. Only the animal's feet were tied. Yet it lay perfectly docile on the wheelbarrow, unmindful of the crowd.

"Is the pig dead?" I asked our guide.

"Oh, no," she said. "The farmer sewed the pig's eyelids together so it cannot see."

Farther down the street an old woman clad in blue, with a leathery face and gnarled hands, carried a heavy load of foot-long red radishes in a basket strapped to her back. Carefree children wearing brightly colored embroidered and appliqued caps with earflaps played in the streets. Little boys and girls alike were dressed in trousers split in the crotch and back, styled for quick action, eliminating the need for diapers.

Down by the canal were the fishermen with their cormorants, or "snakebirds," so called for their long snakelike necks. They fish in the lake at night, hanging lanterns over the side of the boat to attract the fish. The sharp-eyed birds perch on the front of the boat watching for a fish to break water. Then the cormorant plunges in to give chase. Fast swimmers, the birds sometime dive fifty feet in pursuit of their quarry. The bird swims back to the boat with the fish half swallowed, hindered by a small brass ring on its long neck. The fisherman shakes the choking bird upside down. The fish falls out into the boat. And the unhappy bird goes back after another fish. To keep the bird motivated, with every seventh fish the metal ring is removed and the bird finally gets a well-deserved meal!

Vinegar Joe's Road

"That is the end of the Burma Road," Ms. Wei told us, pointing to a gravel road twisting up around a mountainside on the outskirts of the city.

For the moment, history took a geographical focus. We stood there recalling the days of World War II, America's alliance with the Nationalist government of Chiang Kaishek and our war with the Japanese. Kunming was the terminus of the famous Burma Road and the U.S. Air Transport Command's famous "hump" route over the lofty, mist-shrouded mountains of India. The city became a throbbing wartime base, and many Americans saw service in this remote Chinese city.

The 717-mile mountain highway was built to link Burma and China during the Sino-Japanese War that broke out in 1937. The Japanese had occupied all of China's seacoast and were driving inland. For three years the Burma Road was a vital military corridor into China from the outside world. Then the Japanese overran Burma in April 1942 and closed the road.

By that time, both China and the United States were at war with Japan. The reopening of a road into China became a wartime priority. The legendary "Vinegar Joe" Stilwell was given the task. General Stilwell was already Chiang Kaishek's chief of staff. Under "Vinegar Joe," in two years and two months, U.S. Army engineers built a 478-mile road from Assam, India, across the incredibly high and almost impassable Patkai range of the Himalaya Mountains. The road snaked up and down mountainsides, through bogs, swamps, and forests, finally to connect with the old Burma Road in the north. It was one of the most remarkable engineering feats of the war. When opened, the highway was named "The Stilwell Road."

The Allies continued to feed war materials into Kunming, "flying the hump" from the base in Assam 510 miles away. The "Flying Boxcars" lifted an average of fifty thousand tons a months over the treacherous mountain range in an around-the-clock operation. The consistently clear weather and the brilliantly blue, cloudless skies of Kunming, the city of eternal spring, were a significant factor in their success.

The First Christians

When Marco Polo came through Kunming seven centuries ago, he reported seeing "a few Christians . . . who are Nestorians."[2] In the centuries to follow, they totally disappeared.

In the last century, Kunming was designated a treaty port and opened to foreign trade. The city was the inland gateway to the interior of southwest China, 400 miles from the Gulf of Tonkin. In 1910 a narrow-gauge railroad was completed linking Kunming to the south with the key French Indochina city of Hanoi. The commerce and communication via this railroad in time gave Kunming a thin veneer of French culture.

As in Vietnam, French Catholic missionaries were the first to bring Christianity to Kunming in the modern era. In the earlier days, very few American Protestant missionaries came to Kunming. A visitor to the city in 1935 said that he found only a handful of Americans. There was one missionary family with ten children. The worldwide depression had dried up their support, and they were compelled to beg on the streets to survive.[3]

With the Japanese invasion of China, Kunming was thrust into prominence. Chinese fleeing the Japanese troops moved whole factories, industries, and institutions, along with the people, to Kunming to be beyond the range of the Japanese bombers. Then came the influx of Americans in their support of Chiang's Nationalist Army to wage war against the Japanese. This opened Kunming to a brief flurry of Christian mission activity. But after 1949 the story of Christianity in Kunming and Yunnan province is the same as in Guangxi as recounted in the last chapter. On my first visit to Kunming, I found no Christian churches, but the Buddhist temples were open.

Buddha's Red Bag

"Bring your sins and troubles to Buddha," said Ms. Wei, our guide. "He will put them in a big red bag and give you peace and rest," she said in explaining the significance of the red cloth-covered balls that hung in the entryway of the Golden Temple.

"Only the very old Chinese people are religious. These other people in the Temple are tourists, like you," Ms. Wei commented. "Educated Chinese are atheists. We do not believe in religion."

The temple was thick with incense, which swirled up from a massive three-legged brass bowl filled with sand. A somber monk dressed in a seedy red robe stood nearby with a smoky oil lamp in one hand and a fistful of bamboo sticks in the other. The sticks, tipped with a dried compound of sawdust and fragrant oil, looked like tiny cattail spikes. As we watched, the monk impassively handed a burning incense stick to an aged woman. She carefully stuck it in the sand in a miniature forest of smoldering and burned-out sticks.

"Superstitious people believe incense pleases the gods," Ms. Wei said. "Sometimes they even burn paper money as an offering."

The Golden Buddha at the central altar serenely looked down on an occasional worshiper kneeling in prayer on the worn velvet cushions. During the ritual of meditation and prayer, the worshiper's hands were folded and fingers positioned into various postures. Each hand sign had a name and was associated with a particular saint to whom the prayer was addressed. The ornately carved doors, granite columns, and multicolored tilework of the Golden Temple were silent testimonies of the architectural genius of the past and a consuming religious devotion that had long since died.

"The government is restoring the temples," Ms. Wei said and quickly added, "because they are beautiful historical monuments."

Dragon Chasers

North of Kunming, Western Mountain rises straight up two thousand feet. Across the precipitous solid rock face of the cliff Buddhist monks ten centuries ago cut steps upward and built the famous Temples of Western Cloud. No fewer than twenty temples cling precariously to the jagged side of the mountain.

At the entrance of one temple, a ferocious twenty-foot-high "demon chaser" was stationed to frighten away evil spirits. The blue-glazed figure glared ominously with bug-eyes popping, teeth bared, and an upraised left hand brandishing a bronze spear. Inside were the gilded and gaudily painted statutes of various gods of the Buddhist pantheon.

An old monk tended the temple. His shaven head was branded with tonsure marks, deep scars that represented the vows he had taken. With him was a young abbot in training to become a "saint" and gain salvation in Nirvana.

Finding a Lost God

We were staying at the Kunming Hotel, an old landmark without amenities, but clean, comfortable, and with an excellent cuisine of famous spicy Yunnan recipes. Mushrooms were in season. We ate at least a dozen different dishes of fungi—boiled, fried, and mixed with other foods. But the specialty was the famous Yunnan ham, the Chinese equivalent of our smoked salt-cured Kentucky country ham.

A gracious Mr. Chang Li Dao was the hotel's public relations man responsible for dealing with tourists. He spoke fluent English and was ever solicitous of our welfare. In the evening after dinner, he called me aside to talk privately. Pointing to the tiny gold cross I was wearing, he asked, "Why do you wear that?"

"That is a Christian cross. I am a believer," I answered simply.

Mr. Chang hesitated, then timorously asked, "Do you have a Bible that I could read tonight?"

"Only in English," I replied.

"That would be wonderful!" he exclaimed. I took him the Bible and returned to my room.

At breakfast the next morning, Mr. Chang was waiting to greet me. He took me into a side corridor behind a black lacquered screen. There, with unchecked joy and emotion, he said, "I stayed awake all night reading the Bible. I had lost my God but now I have found Him again."

With intense feeling, Mr. Chang told me his story. He was from Sichuan Province, to the north, where he was educated in a Christian missionary school. His father and mother were both Christians. He was converted as a teenager, but he had "fallen away" in his twenties. Since then he had been living without God in his life. He was very miserable. The death of his father three years ago had depressed him greatly. "But now, God has come back into my heart and I will never leave him again," he passionately declared.

I asked Mr. Chang if he knew of any other Christians in Kunming. He paused as if a debate were going on inside him and then said, "Yes."

"I would like so very much to meet them," I said.

He shook his head. "I don't know. Maybe."

That morning, we left the hotel going southwest across the Kunming plateau into the mountains toward the Vietnam border. We drove by scattered villages and through quaint valleys studded with terraced rice fields. We passed clumsy water buffalo pulling big two-wheeled carts. Along the roadside was the ever-present peasant shuffling along in a rhythmic gait with two burdened baskets swinging from a shoulder pole. Occasionally we saw a woman or child sitting by the road selling mushrooms freshly picked in the forests.

We stopped for pictures of farmers working in the rice paddies.

"The seed are first soaked in water to help them sprout," Ms. Wei explained. "Then they are sown in a nursery plot." We were watching a work crew of men and women, knee-deep in water, transplanting five-inch seedlings. Continuously bent over, they slowly moved in a line across the field, with a bundle of seedlings in one hand and sticking the plants deep into the mud with the other. When the rice is mature the fields are drained. Then, stalk by stalk, the grain heads are cut off by hand.

"Isn't there machinery to do this?" asked a Georgia farmer in our group.

"Yes," Wei explained, "but we have many people and few machines. And, besides, if we used machinery, all these people would have no jobs."

The Stone Forest

We came out of the valley plateau into the mountains to the famous Stone Forest. It is an extraordinary sight, a spectacular panorama of jagged, misshapen rock obelisks, some as tall as California redwoods. The treelike stone formations covered hundreds of acres, intermingled with arches, caves, and crystal-clear pools. Geologists explain that this area was once submerged, an ancient lake, and the action of the water cut these formations as the water receded.

Near the Forest of Stone Trees is the mountain village of Wulouke inhabited by the Yi, another of China's national minorities. On the streets of Kunming we had seen some of the minority people of this region, Miao tribesmen in their curious black dresses, fur-hatted white-robed Lolo from Tibet, and Yi women in red turban-like hats and brilliant blue and pink woven dresses.

In times past, the minority peoples of this region lived in abject and indescribable poverty. A visitor in the late 1930s gave this account of one village: "They were so poor that the women would not emerge from their huts. They had no clothes. They sat huddled in nakedness beside the straw cooking fire. Girls of seventeen and eighteen worked naked in the fields. Many families had only one pair of trousers to share among three or four adult males."[4]

These minority peoples generally have been despised and mistreated by the Han Chinese in the past. The written symbol for "dog" was always attached to their ethnic name. They were called "Dog-Miao" or "Dog-Lolo" or "Dog-Yi."

"This practice is forbidden today," Ms. Wei assured us. We were told that the government has a special university for the training of the minorities. They are free to maintain their native languages and customs. Their civil rights are protected. They are exempt from the national birth-control policy that limits other Chinese to one child per family.

The Yi

The Yi are the largest minority group in this part of China, numbering five million in all. They are tall, dark, and distinctively un-Chinese. The Yi came into this area from somewhere out of the northwest, Burma and Tibet, long before the Han Chinese appeared. They were fierce warriors who attacked neighboring groups to capture wives and slaves.

The Yi were a slave-owning aristocratic society with numerous social grades. Slaves had slaves. Two centuries before Christ, the Han Chinese appeared and, in time, drove the Yi into the mountains where they eked out a meager living by herding, hunting, and primitive "hoe-using" farming.

In the past, this was opium country. Everyone age fifteen and above smoked opium. Men, women, and teenagers with glazed eyes sat outside their huts puffing their pipes. Opium smoke was blown into infants' nostrils when they were sick to make them well or to ease their discomfort. Thus children sometimes became addicted by the time they were walking. Opium was the principal cash crop of the mountain farmers. Visitors in the villages reported seeing opium piled in brown stacks in the sheds like cow dung put out to dry.[5]

Fiercely independent, even into the middle of this century, the Yi resisted the authority of the warlords who ruled the valleys and the Nationalist and Communist armies. Banditry was an honorable way of life, and any outsider was fair game. The Communist regime has finally "pacified" the Yi and brought them into the structure of orderly society.

We visited a village of Sani, a subgrouping of the Yi. It was a complex of red adobe houses, walls, and compounds. As we walked through the village, the open areas were full of children, chickens, dogs, and native pigs (black, swaybacked, with huge bellies that scraped the ground, spindly legs, and undeveloped hams).

"They are very superstitious people," Ms. Wei said pointing to a long pole with a talisman of rag, corn shucks, and a piece of metal tied at the top. "That is to keep the evil spirits away from the house. They believe there are spirits and gods in everything, plants, trees, rocks, the streams, the night, the day." Their religion is a mixture of animism and Buddhism, and every village has its own shaman (or priest).

A Witness to the Minorities

On the way back to Kunming, I thought about these tribal people of China, a nation within a nation, 67 million of them. That is more than the population of Italy, the United Kingdom, Canada, the Philippines, or Turkey. Only eleven nations in the world are larger than this body of "national minorities" within China!

All foreign mission work with the minorities ended in 1949. But the Chinese Christians now feel the burden of spiritual concern for them. Dr. C. K. Chang, a Christian professor at Anhui University in Wuhu, told me, "I have a graduate who is a doctor working among the Miao and Zhuang. He cannot preach because he is a doctor. But he is a very fervent witness and tells all his patients about Jesus Christ. In fact, throughout the region, he is known as 'The Christian Doctor' and is highly respected. He has a sense of calling to the tribal peoples. Many have been won by his witness."[6]

David Y. K. Wong also told me of the dedication of many Chinese Christians to carry the gospel to the remote areas. "There are many 'Bible Women' and 'Women Evangelists' who are very dedicated to the Gospel mission. I know of one particular woman preacher. When she was eighteen years old, she dedicated her life to Christian work. During the Cultural Revolution she was arrested and spent seven years at hard labor. But now, she has been released. Today she travels from village to village in remote areas preaching to two hundred and three hundred people at a time. Farmers come from miles away, carrying their simple food with them, to attend the meetings. This Bible woman often must speak six times a day, the people are so hungry for the gospel. She told me in an assured and confident manner that she sees the beginning of a great revival in China today."[7]

At the hotel that evening after dinner, my newfound friend, Mr. Chang, the hotel's public relations man, led me down the hall to a small room off the lobby.

"Hungry eyes will not see us in here," he said as he opened the door. Two men, seated in the room, rose to greet me. "These are your brothers in the family of Jesus here in Kunming."

For the next two hours we talked as Mr. Chang interpreted. They were members of a house church. The older man had been a Christian from before the revolution. The young man, a university student, was a recent convert.

That was in 1980 when I made this first contact with the house churches. They told me many stories of how the house churches began, how these secret groups met privately and sometimes at tremendous risk. Sometimes it was a single family. Sometimes a small prayer group of Christian women would gather together. They met irregularly but not infrequently at different houses for prayer meetings, Bible study, and fellowship. They said, "We have won many souls . . . found God a great help in time of trouble . . . prayed together . . . no set form for the meeting . . . very spontaneous . . . usually short." They said the authorities prohibited religious meetings in private homes during the Cultural Revolution. If more than two persons were found praying together at home, they were liable for prosecution as counterrevolutionaries and faced possible imprisonment.

Twenty-Five Million Believers

Since 1980 I have watched the emergence of these "silent ones," the secret and clandestine house groups. With the restoration of religious freedom under the new regime, the secret house churches slowly became open gatherings. Christians united to form congregations and lay claim to confiscated church properties and were reestablished as open independent churches, adhering to the Three-Self principle. In 1986 there are four thousand open Three-Self Protestant churches in China with four million members.

At the same time, tens of thousands of house churches still meet apart from these open churches. Estimates of the number of believers in the house churches range from as few as five million to an unbelievable one hundred million.

Several "China Watchers" associated with religious organizations in Hong Kong and the United States put the figures at fifty million, almost 5 percent of the population. "Most Sino-missiologists believe that twenty million Protestant Christians in these 'house gatherings' is a reliably conservative figure," says Southern Baptist Lewis Myers.[8]

House churches are reported in all of China's twenty-two provinces and five autonomous and three metropolitan districts. Areas of most rapid growth are in the southern coastal provinces of Zhejiang, Fujian, and Guangdong, as well as interior Sichuan and Henan. Extensive growth also is reported in Inner Mongolia.

Thomas Wang describes the house churches as grass-roots fellowships interested in person-to-person evangelism. They are independent and spreading fast in China today. They treasure their freedom of preaching the gospel. They are spontaneous expressions of New Testament Christianity.

"If the father of a home is converted, he is zealous for the gospel and immediately starts a meeting in his home. He automatically becomes the leader. He begins to teach and preach even though he has been a Christian for only three months."[9]

"In the present atmosphere there is no longer any reason for house churches to be clandestine or to meet secretly," observed Arne Sovik of the Lutheran World Federation.[10] These groups vary in size from ten to two thousand. The larger groups meet in public places. They may meet outdoors in yards, fields, or tents, and public places with the full knowledge of local officials. Today it is inaccurate to identify the house churches of China as an underground church. Bishop K. H. Ting, chairman of the China Christian Council and the Three-Self Committee, has repeatedly said, "The government extends official recognition to all these groups."

An Adventist couple from the United States teaches English in a Chinese university. They worship regularly in a house church near the university (because there is no organized church in the area). The Americans don't speak Chinese. The Chinese don't speak English. "Yet we have a satisfying spiritual fellowship. First we hum the tunes of a few hymns until we find a melody all of us know. Then we sing them together—they in Chinese and we in English. Next we select a text or two. They read it from the Chinese Bible and we from the English. Finally we have prayer, with each praying in his own tongue." A few years ago, such a service would have been unthinkable.[11]

"It is not 'either/or,'" Mr. Han Wenzao of Nanjing told me in regard to the house church versus the open church. "We need both. When we put up a church building, it is a witness to the whole city. It arouses curiosity and interest. It causes people to raise questions and to 'come and see.' Christians are a small minority in China, and we need all the publicity and advertising we can get. Also, Christians need to gather in groups to hear sermons, to learn and grow. The Chinese people like long sermons, an hour or more. The Chinese are Bible-loving people. They are eager to hear the Bible explained."[12]

On the other hand, many people have found a new spiritual life-style in the small home congregations. Their faith has been deepened by the new intimacy not realized in the larger public meetings. "They find a special fulfillment in participation in the small group," a pastor told me.

The hard reality is that the house churches are a necessity because there are not enough open facilities to accommodate all the believers in China, and there will not be adequate facilities any time in the immediate future.

There are many times more Protestant Christians today than thirty years ago. Christian groups worship in many new places where, previously, there were no church buildings. There are at least twenty thousand more places of worship in homes, schools, and houses than there were churches in existence thirty years ago. Even if all church facilities were immediately returned to the house congregations awaiting facilities, "there still wouldn't be enough churches to accommodate the present number of Christians," observed Arne Sovik.[13]

Protestant Christianity in China has exploded in the house churches while Catholic Christianity has declined. The papal requirement that Chinese Catholics maintain an alliance to Rome has been a significant factor in their decline.

Another explanation for this difference between Catholic and Protestant growth lies in their contrasting ecclesiology. In the Catholic Church power and authority moves from the top down through the church structure with special authority given the priesthood. Proper authority is required to conduct the mass, to teach the Bible, and to lead worship. Laity are primarily participants.

Protestants, on the other hand, are congregational in structure. Authority generates from the congregation up. Protestants are not dependent upon an external priestly anointment for authority to carry on priestly functions. Consequently leadership rises from the ranks to conduct worship and perform other churchly functions.

As churches were closed in China, Catholics did not have the traditional structure in which to practice their faith. Catholics had limited leadership to conduct their services, teach the Bible, and mediate their prayers. Some Catholics continued to meet in house churches. But many "fell away," and some even sought fellowship with Protestant believers in small home groups where they ultimately lost their identity as Catholics.

As we were departing Kunming, Mr. Chang Li Dao came to bid us good-bye. With deep emotion he took my hand and said, "It is so wonderful, what has happened to me. Like the Bible says, 'You have sown the seed.' Yes, the seed will sprout and produce manyfold. I hope you come back to see the many fruits of the gospel seed that have been sown in Kunming."

Seed! Jesus said, "The kingdom of heaven is like . . . a sower who goes forth to sow." The seed is the gospel. A hotel employee receives a Bible. . . . a Christian doctor treats a Miao Tribesman in the hills. . . . a Bible Woman preaches in a remote village. . . . a university student is invited to a family prayer meeting. . . . seed bringing forth fruit a hundredfold!

Notes

1. The "house churches" or home gatherings of China are in the tradition of early New Testament Christianity. The apostle Paul wrote, "Salute . . . Nymphas, and the church which is in his house" (Col. 4:15) and "To Philemon our beloved fellow worker . . . and to the church in your house" (Philem. 1, RSV). The church in Jerusalem met in the house of Mary (Acts 12:12); the church at Philippi, in the house of Lydia (Acts 16:40); the church at Ephesus, in the house of Aquila and Priscilla (1 Cor. 16:19) and later in their home at Rome (Rom. 16:5). As the Christian "sacrifices" were spiritual and required no temple, Christians did not haste to erect buildings for public worship. It was not until the third century that Christians built structures specifically to house worshiping congregations.

2. For information about the Nestorians, see Chapter 6 and the story of Alopen.

3. E. J. Kahn, Jr., *The China Hands* (New York: Viking, 1975), p. 57.

4. Harrison E. Salisbury, *The Long March* (New York: Harper and Row, 1985), a personal interview with Yu Quili, p. 106.

5. Ibid., p. 107.

6. From a personal interview with Dr. C. K. Chang, professor of English, Anhui Normal University, Wuhu, East China.

7. Dr. David Y. K. Wong is a past president of the Baptist World Alliance. He was born in Canton, was a successful architect and businessman in Hong Kong, and now lives in California.

8. Dr. Lewis Myers, Cooperative Services International, Richmond, Virginia.

9. Thomas Wang in a report to World Evangelization, September 6, 1986, 44, 13:5-6. Lausanne Committee for World Evangelization, P.O. Box 2308, Charlotte, N.C. 28211.

10. *The Bridge* 7 (October 1980).

11. Alf Lohne, "China Report" *Ministry Magazine,* September 1980.

12. Personal interview with Mr. Han Wenzao.

13. *The Bridge*.

5

The Pepper Pots

Chengdu (Chengtu)

"I may never see you again in this life," I said, waving my handkerchief to the Chinese congregation and pointing up. "But we shall see each other in heaven." They sealed the covenant with a sea of handkerchiefs and upraised fingers. I had explained that fellow believers in Russia taught me this farewell.

"There are Christians in Russia?" my translator, Pastor Hua Chang-chi, asked in disbelief.

"Many hundreds of thousands in over five thousand churches. I have preached to them in many places in Russia. We shall all see each other again in heaven."

"No! No!" Pastor Hua protested. "We will see you here again. God will bring you back." That was 1980 in Chengdu, the capital of Sichuan Province. Here I had my first experience in a Chinese worship service. The church had been reopened one month earlier.

"Texanic Sichuan"

Our flight had taken us over the mist-shrouded Ta-lou Shan mountain range into a vast inland basin, the "rice basket" of China. The terraced hillsides extended as far as the eye could see. This was Sichuan Province, often called "Land of a Million Steps." The paddies full of water shimmered in the sun like a mosaic of broken mirrors. Farther out on the plateau the rivers, streams, and irrigation ditches twisted through the fields and forests, making a crazy quilt pattern of browns and greens. We were flying over the fabulously fertile Chengdu plain.

"Welcome to Chengdu," Mr. Lieu, our guide, greeted us as we deplaned.

En route to the venerable Jinjiang Hotel, Lieu gave a Chamber-of-Commerce introduction to the city. "The Chinese call Chengdu *Tien Fu Chih Kuo,* meaning 'Heaven on Earth.'" Here everything was bigger and better than anywhere else in China. But for his Oriental features Lieu could have been a Texan introducing us to Dallas!

In fact, there are similarities between Sichuan and Texas, Chengdu and Dallas. Both are geographically isolated in the deep southwestern region of their country. Both are rich in natural resources, affluent and showy in their wealth. Both have a tradition, history, and pride all their own. Both are spectacularly big by every measurement.

Sichuan is a country within a country; it is China's most populous province with 104 million people. If the province were a nation, Sichuan would be the world's eighth largest.

Sichuan has a spectacular and unmatched variety of geography. The mighty Yangtze gathers her waters from the vast plateau in four tributaries. (Sichuan means "four rivers" in Chinese.) In her rush eastward to the sea, the Yangtze gathers momentum to slice a precipitous 150-mile canyon through the rugged Wu Shan mountain range, creating the bold and awesome Yangtze gorges.

To the west, on the Tibetan borderlands, lay the "Great Snowy" Mountains whose frigid peaks average three miles in height.

To the south, the River of Golden Sands cuts a serpentine course through isolated mountains. From antiquity the inhabitants have panned for gold in her sandy bars.

Here is the home of the giant panda, the rare golden monkey, and the Ling Yang, a mountain deer whose musk glands produce the ingredient for the most precious perfumes.

The province is rimmed with mountains rich in minerals and slopes abundant with timber. Sichuan leads all China in the production of rice, wheat, sweet potatoes, and rape seed.

The Pepper Pots

"Texanic" Chengdu is a dynamic city of 3.75 million people. From medieval times the city was renowned for its fine silks, brocades, and rich and opulent culture. Chengdu was on the ancient "Silk Road" to Europe. In the tenth century her merchants invented the use of paper money in commerce.

Distance and isolation imprinted the people of this region with a distinctively identifiable personality. Sophisticated and urbane, a person from Chengdu is characteristically gregarious, aggressive, independent, outspoken, and a free thinker. We found our guide, Lieu, fully open, relaxed, jovial, and flexible.

The renowned Sichuan cuisine is also "Texanic." It is ma-la-tang, which means "numbing spicy and scalding hot." The tiny Sichuan pepper-corns are mixed with strips of chicken, pork, and vegetables in a hundred different ways that are guaranteed to satisfy the cast-iron stomach of the most avid Texas chili gourmet. Fortified with a pocketful of antacid tables, a Westerner finds the menus of Sichuan a memorable delight.

Throughout China a person from Sichuan Province is nicknamed "Pepper Pot" because of his taste for hot foods and his fiery personality.

"Sichuan is the home of Deng Xiaoping," Lieu told us with pride.

The peppery Deng is an independent, free-thinking spirit, and his Sichuan plainspokenness continually kept him in trouble with the authoritarian Mao. Although twice exiled by Mao for his capitalistic ideas, Deng had the resiliency of an India rubber ball and bounced back both times, ultimately to head the most popular regime in China since the peak of Mao's popularity in the early 1950s.

Time magazine selected Deng as "Man of the Year" in 1985 for "introducing China's sweeping economic reforms which have challenged Marxist orthodoxies and liberated the productive energies of a billion people."[1]

The Bottom Line

Sichuan Province was the seedbed for Deng's economic and political reforms. Here Deng's protege, Governor Zhao Ziyang (who later became China's premier) initially experimented with the concepts that would become the basis of the new reforms: decentralization, economic freedom, free market forces, compensation in proportion to production and quality of work, individual responsibility. Economic results, and not doctrinaire consistency, were to be the bottom line. The final test of socialism's validity was to be pragmatic, not ideological.

Deng had other simple objectives besides getting the farmers producing and the factories running efficiently. He was determined to rectify the injustices of the Cultural Revolution (in which he and his family had suffered greatly) and to give justice to the victims. One practical spin-off was the full recognition of the individual citizen's right to the freedom of worship and the return of church properties to the congregations. The government also was to reimburse the churches with rent for the use of the confiscated property.

"It is good that the churches are opening again," Lieu said. He acknowledged he was not religious, but "Religious people are honest, hard workers, moral, and that is good for society."

It was Sunday morning, and we were on our way to church. As our bus turned out of the hotel gates down the broad Renmin Avenue toward the central square, Lieu continued. "There were American, British, Canadian and Australian missionaries in Chengdu. They did many good things for the Chinese people." He pointed across from the hotel. "I was educated in a missionary high school right there." Pointing back across the Nan River beyond our hotel, he said, "That was a missionary hospital, a medical school, and West China Union University. it is now Sichuan Medical College."

As we approached the town square, there on a pedestal stood the twenty-foot statue of Mao, bareheaded, solemn-faced, right hand raised as in a papal blessing, left hand tucked behind his back, his long army overcoat blown open by an unseen breeze.

"Would Mao approve the changes Deng is making in China?" I asked Lieu.

"Mao is dead," Lieu answered simply. "Today we have a new China."

One in the Spirit

A few blocks to the right and up a side street we found the large stone-walled church compound. A stately white-haired woman, the senior pastor's wife, Mrs. Hsu Yao Kwuan, greeted us at the gate. The courtyard was already full of people thirty minutes before church time. Many of the congregation were already in the sanctuary practicing the hymns to be sung in the service, for there were few hymnbooks and many of the older people could not read.

"This was an Anglican church and the bishop's headquarters," Mrs. Hsu said as we continued on to the manse.

"I am a Baptist too," Hsu Yao Kwuan, the senior pastor, said as he took my hand. Pastor Hsu was tall, with a fatherly countenance, a square face, sharp eyes, and a gray blocky crew cut. We sipped tea and visited for a few minutes. With us was Wallace Wang, also a Baptist. He had studied at Union Theological Seminary in the United States and was professor of New Testament in the West China College before 1949. Hua Chang-Chi was to be my interpreter. Then there was the charming woman minister Yen I Chen. In all, the church had six pastors, two Baptists, two Church of Christ of China, one Canadian Methodist, and one from the China Inland Mission.

"But we are all one in the Spirit now," Pastor Hsu declared.

Wallace Wang said that the church had only been open one month. We were the first foreign visitors.

We filed across the courtyard and into the church. The black lacquered pews were packed. Chairs were set in the aisles. People crowded at the windows, looking in. One third of the congregation were young people. A red velvet hanging with a white cross in the center was on the wall behind the simple pulpit. Above it was the single word *Hallelujah*.

"The Ten Commandments are to the left and the Lord's Prayer to the right," said Hua, explaining the wall panels that flanked the pulpit.

As the wheezing organ played softly, Hua put a Chinese hymnal into my hand, open to page 1, and pointed to the incomprehensible characters.

The sound of hundreds of voices raising in song filled the simple sanctuary. I looked around at the radiant faces. They were singing with total abandonment. I recognized the song and something melted within me. Suddenly I was one with them. Bar by bar, phrase by phrase, I joined in singing. English and Chinese blended in: "Holy, Holy, Holy, Lord God Almighty!"

The stately black-robed Pastor Hsu stepped to the pulpit with Bible in hand. In a rich mellow voice he read, " 'In the beginning was the Word. And the Word became flesh and dwelt among us.' In the flesh Jesus was a Jew. But in the Spirit He was the universal almighty God. Jesus was 'God with us.' "

"There are many university students here and he is explaining to them who Jesus is," Hua whispered. Hsu prayed and then we all prayed the Lord's Prayer, English and Chinese mixed in perfect harmony. We were the family of God talking to our Father.

The offertory hymn was "Whiter than Snow." I could not sing for watching the people around me. One elderly lady on the same pew wept silently. Nearby, a young man threw back his head, fixed his eyes upward, and sang, "Lord Jesus, I long to be perfectly whole." The singing began to slow down, slower and slower, richer in emotion, steadily falling behind the organ. The last three bars were sung a capella.

The offering was received in a black velvet bag with a wooden handle. Giving was an entirely private matter. Each person thrust a clenched fist into the bag and released an offering known only by God.

Salt

Although Pastor Hsu was seventy-seven years old, he preached a powerful sermon. His voice was melodious and displayed a full range of rich tones. He was warm, articulate, emotional. As I received the message through a translator, I felt the full impact of the pastor's sincerity and the sense of urgency in his pleading. His text was, "Ye are the salt of the earth." "Christians are salt," Hua whispered softly in my ear, "of the earth . . . that means world. All over the world Christians are working like salt . . . regardless of political situations or social structures. Without salt meat decays . . . food is tasteless . . . society without Christ decays . . . life without Christ is tasteless."

Then, as we stood and sang "More Love to Thee, O Christ," I felt a great surge of spiritual power. I had been on holy ground. During the benediction I thought of all the bitter years of oppression, the untold sufferings of many of these people who were now singing praises to God.

With tears in my eyes, I looked up to the altar at the one word, *Hallelujah*.

Hua touched my arm and signaled for me to follow the pastors out of the sanctuary. Then he stopped on the steps and said, "It was not proper to ask you to speak in the church. But here outside we would like to hear from you." As the congregation gathered in the courtyard, I brought greetings from their Christian brothers and sisters around the world and waved good-bye with my handkerchief and pointed upward, promising to meet them in heaven.

As I pressed through the crowd to the waiting bus, I met smiling students in white shirts, girls in bright-colored blouses, white-haired saints with misty eyes, shy young children, dapper young men in Western suits, rough-handed laborers in worn blue jackets and pants, all a part of my newfound family of faith in Chengdu.

Subduing the Dragon

A giant dragon lived at the bottom of the river. He devoured the land and the people with great floods. Every year a little child was sacrificed to appease the dragon's anger. But a great king, Li Bing, ingeniously disguised himself, appeared before the dragon, and subdued him. After that, the king built this dam and irrigation system. This was the story of Li Bing, who built the mammoth Chengdu irrigation system two hundred years before Christ.

We had driven twenty-five miles northwest of the city to see the Du Jiang Yan Dam that harnessed the Min River and made an agricultural paradise of 16 1/2 million acres of the Chengdu basin.

The turbulent Min (one of the four tributaries of the mighty Yangtze) plunges from the Sichuan ranges in such volume that it is not unusual for the water to rise twenty feet in a twenty-four hour period. Li Bing cut a trunk channel though a solid granite mountain to siphon off the floodwaters. Without explosives or machinery, construction workers heated the rock, doused it with water, and slowly chipped it away. A massive dam was built to store the water, which was then fed into a series of fingers, spillways, and sluices. The sluiceway delivered the water around a bend in such a way as to cause the silt-laden water to flow slower in a deep diversionary channel, while the faster and cleaner surface water was carried into the irrigation ditches.

Atop Green City Mountain, overlooking this vast project, a four-ton statue of Li Bing stands in the Dragon Subduing Taoist Temple. Visitors burn incense sticks before his statue as Taoist monks tend the temple.

For centuries Taoism was the official religion of China. Basically a philosophical approach to life, it teaches that through nature "The Great Way" is found. Taoism emphasizes the achievement of serenity and perfect adjustment in life by the elimination of striving and conflict.

Traditionally, non-Christian Chinese generally did not maintain rigid boundaries of religious belief. Many Chinese Taoists would play it safe by also being a Confucianist and Buddhist, at the same time. Often, burning incense is not so much an act of worship as paying tribute to an ancestor or a great person, just as Westerners place flowers on a grave without any particular religious significance.

Tai Ji

"That is called Tai Ji," Lieu explained as we left the hotel early the next morning. In a park by the river more than one hundred people were engaged in the Chinese version of aerobics, a balletlike slow-motion exercise like shadow boxing. It was not organized, each doing his own thing, gracefully lifting a foot, stretching arms, crouching, posturing. This ancient form of calisthentics, accompanied by certain mental exercises, is a ritual based on Taoist philosophy to get the conflicting forces of yin and yang in harmony and bring health to the body and well-being to the spirit.

We were soon through the city and into the countryside. The twisting, narrow roads were crowded with commerce. Hand carts were piled high with fodder. Walking tractors pulled small trailers filled with gravel, cement, and lumber. People carried big wicker baskets of farm produce. There were tricycles and bicycles galore. It is amazing what a bicycle can carry strapped behind the rider: a trussed-up live pig, a slatted coop of chickens or ducks, boxes piled ten feet high, huge bundles of wheat straw, and even a kitchen table. We passed lush fields of corn, rice, wheat, barley, and yellow-flowered rape plants. Scattered about were clusters of thatched, mud-brick farm houses shaded by elegant bamboos and spreading banyan trees.

Sichuan Province is 87 percent rural, with the world's densest agrarian population. Mao's "great leap forward," followed by the Cultural Revolution, wrecked the economy of this richly endowed granary. When Mao died, Sichuan was failing to feed itself and had to import grain.

Agriculture was at the top of the list of Deng's four modernizations. He had to get the farmers to produce again, no matter what the cost. We were on our way to visit a rice commune that was one of the pilot projects that radically changed Chinese agriculture and ultimately all of Chinese life.

The Commune

Originally the basic organization of the Communist economic structure was the commune. In the city, it was a factory. In rural areas, it was usually based upon the old pre-1949 agricultural village. The areas to be farmed by the commune could be anywhere from fifteen to several thousand acres. There were fifty thousand such communes in China, averaging sixteen thousand members each.

The commune was broken down into brigades averaging about 2,000 people, or 450 households. In turn, the brigades were broken down into production teams of 150 to 200 people, or 30 to 40 families. Each production team was given a specific labor assignment under the supervision of a team leader. The commune was to be a self-contained unit providing and operating a clinic and a school for the constituency.

Deng Xiaoping contended that the production teams were too large to be efficient and that Central Planning was not working. The emphasis was shifted to individual workers. Land was reassigned to individual family groups. The terminology began to change, from *commune* to *co-operative*. The industrial commune began to be called a factory or a company.

The rice commune's headquarters was a flat-roofed, one-story, concrete building. We were ushered into a meeting room and took our seats in chairs around the wall. As we were served steaming mugs of tea, a tanned, leathery-faced official told us about the rice commune.

"Before liberation this rice plantation belonged to wealthy landlords. Now it belongs to the people. Two thousand families make up the commune. The commune is assigned a production quota of rice by the government. Under the old system when everyone worked together and was paid the same wage, we always had difficulty meeting the quota," he said.

"Now, under the new system, the land is divided up. Family units sign contracts for specific plots of land. If they produce more than their quota, they earn bonus points. Now everyone works harder to produce more, to earn bonus points and receive more money. With more money they buy radios, bicycles, furniture, or move into a nice apartment. Some even earn enough to build a new house.

"Under the new policy, the commune is free to expand into other money-making projects. We planted mulberry trees on the levees between the rice fields to feed silkworms. Now the commune has a silk thread factory. We grow rape and produce vegetable oil. The surplus rice, the silk thread, and the rape seed oil are sold on the open market. We pay a tax to the government on the extra income. Profits are divided on the basis of production bonus points, and some profits are used to increase the social services to the people.

"Individuals are also free to engage in profit-making sidelines. They may grow vegetables, raise livestock, chickens, and ducks, and make handicraft items to sell on the free market," concluded the official.

"Some of these farmers are getting very rich," Lieu told us as we were waking to the silk factory. "They have money to buy nice clothes, take vacations, and even travel in China."

As we walked down the path beside a brilliant mustard-colored field of blossoming rape, I tried to sift out what I had just heard. These people are similar to renters or tenant farmers. The state, rather than a corporation or individual, is the landlord. The production quota is their rent. Individuals are not equally compensated but are paid on the basis of their production. The commune is essentially a cooperative owned by the employees, one that can buy and sell surpluses on the open market. Enterprise and entrepreneurism are encouraged, individually and collectively. Making a profit, personal gain, and getting rich are unashamedly the goal of the cooperative, as well as the individual.

The commune had recently completed a two-story apartment complex. We were invited to wander throughout and visit freely with the residents. Each apartment had two rooms that were small by our standards. They were furnished with a bed, table, chairs, and attractively decorated with pictures and mementos. Bicycles were parked in most of the entry halls.

The apartments were ingeniously lighted by methane gas produced from a sealed vat of animal manure and organic matter. Tacked to the wall like an electric cord, a tiny quarter-inch clear plastic tube carried gas up and across the ceiling and down to the globed fixture with an asbestos mantle like a Coleman lantern.

A small kitchen, four by six feet with a tiny window, adjoined the two living rooms. It was equipped with a charcoal brazier, a tiny sink, and a single faucet. On the counter were a cleaver, a cutting board, a wok, a ladle, and two ceramic bowls. A three-foot concrete wall divided the kitchen from the family's private pigsty.

In every apartment we saw from one to six pigs packed in this tiny space. They were not the native pigs I had seen in the Yi village in Kunming. They were highly bred, lean Hampshires. At the slightest sound or movement, they lined up like well-trained soldiers, snouts thrust high and squealing, waiting for scraps from the kitchen. A sloping floor drained the water and manure out through a pipe into the methane gas tank.

Good News in a Teahouse

I was shopping in the huge Exhibition Hall at City Center where the giant statue of Mao stands when a young Chinese woman approached me.

"Are you a bishop?" she asked.

"A pastor," I replied.

"I saw you Sunday at the church, telling about the Russian Christians."

She continued, "My name is Len. I am a university student. A group of us have been discussing Christianity. We were very young during the Cultural Revolution when they destroyed all the Bibles. We do not know anything about the Bible, God, or Jesus. We have been taught to be atheists. But it is not right to hide from us the other side of the question. We have a right to know. If you are a bishop, you could tell us about these things. Maybe tonight?"

That night at the gates of the Jinjiang Hotel, Len and six other young people—medical students, an engineer, a musician, a teacher—were waiting. All spoke English fluently.

"I know a teahouse on Dongfeng Road where we can go," Len said as we boarded the trolley bus for the eastern suburbs.

The teahouse was hardly the legendary "August Moon." It was a large hall, with oilcloth-covered tables and wooden chairs. We pushed tables together in a back corner as Len ordered orange sodas and a watery chocolate drink.

I was bombarded with questions about evolution, the conflict between religion and science, miracles, whether Christians really eat flesh and drink blood!

Finally Len called the group to order and said, "Deliver us a sermon about Christianity."

"Yes, yes," the students said, leaning with elbows on the table, eager, earnest, expectant, yet with a cautious skepticism on their faces.

Climbing Jacob's Ladder

Never have I faced a more challenging assignment. With the teahouse table as a pulpit, drawing on a sheet of paper to make my points and analogies visual, I started at the beginning, the existence of God.

I presented the evidence of "The First Cause." Drawing a series of bricks standing upright in a line I said, "Imagine that I push the first brick over, and, in a chain reaction, all bricks are knocked down." Turning to Xu, the engineering student, I asked, "What toppled the last brick?"

"The brick next to it," he answered. "And that brick?" "The one next to it." "And the first brick?" "You pushed it." I said, "Science goes from effect to cause, but does not explain the first cause, the initial action, the beginning before which there was no other beginning."

Xu quickly answered, "Oh, yes, the beginning was the big bang."

"What caused the 'big bang'?" I asked.

Xu hesitated. "The collision of the positive and negative forces in the atoms, I think."

"What made the positive and negative forces of energy in the atoms?"

He thought a while and then said, "I don't know."

"You see, Xu," I said, "a purely mechanical and physical explanation cannot answer the question of the 'first cause.' Just like the bricks, someone with will, mind, power, and energy that already existed as a distinct personality had to push the first brick." I handed an open Bible to Xu and said, "Read that first sentence."

Xu looked a moment and then slowly read, "In the beginning, God . . . ." There was a frown of incredibility on his face. I could see the gears of his mind trying to synchronize what he had just read with what he had always been taught. His eyes opened wide; he slapped the table and said, "Of course, I see. Why has this never been explained to me?" He took out a note pad and pencil and said, "Wait, I must write all this down. I must not forget any of it." And from that point on, Xu would interrupt again and again, saying, "Wait, I want to write that down."

After that, it was like climbing Jacob's ladder. With every round we went higher and higher.

We talked of "The Watchmaker" argument for the existence of God. The very existence of a watch is evidence of a mind, a designer, a maker, a master craftsman, greater than the watch itself.

We talked of incarnation, how the God of creation could fully reveal Himself to many only by becoming a man among us in Jesus Christ.

We talked of the Bible, not a book about God, but a book from God by revelation, through which He has spoken to us.

We talked of religion. Religion was the upward reach of man for God, but Christianity was the downward reach of God for man.

We had talked for three hours when Len brought the discussion to an end. "I can believe this. I could be a Christian. But I do not want to be a blind Christian. I need help to understand the things I do not know."

It was after midnight. The buses were on a reduced schedule. So we decided to walk back to the hotel together. The streets were empty, the moon was bright, the air cool and fresh. The students began to talk about themselves. They were very bitter about the Cultural Revolution and the last years of Mao's rule.

"We were being told that the commune system was working and life was getting better," one said. "But all the time there was more and more poverty and suffering."

"Now we read that the leaders were lying to us and falsifying production reports," Xu said. He repeated what Len had said in the Exhibition Hall. "We should have the right to read the Bible, just as we have the right to read Karl Marx. Then we should be free to choose what we believe."

I told the students we were leaving early the next morning and bid them good-bye at the Jinjiang gates.

The next morning, as our bus rolled through the hotel gates, there were the students again. They were waving handkerchiefs in the air and pointing to the sky!

Chengdu Postscript

Pastor Hua Chang-chi's prophecy came true. Five years later, God did get me back to Chengdu in the summer of 1985. The changes were unbelievable.

A heavy industrial haze hung over the booming city. New construction was everywhere. It was a bit sad. Many of the quaint centuries-old one-story houses, with their projecting eaves and gracefully curved roofs and elaborate ornaments, were gone. They were demolished to make room for fifteen-story concrete highrise apartments. Now, all the focus is on modernization. At some point in the future, I hope preservationists will step in to conserve something of Chengdu's character and the beauty of Old China.

Downtown was a new world of blue jeans, brightly colored blouses, the click of high heels on pavement, Western suits, billboards touting Japanese radios and Chinese-made brand products, private cars, and red and cream-colored motor bikes. Deng's economic reforms were on the fast track. The vehicle is careening down the road. No one is quite sure where it is going. But no one wants to stop it!

The rural areas are affected too. The people no longer speak of communes, but cooperatives and companies, and customers and exports, and profits, pure and simple. In some areas, 85 percent of the farmers have built their own homes; some of are elaborately decorated three-story villas.

Deng's sweeping reforms in agricultural policy have been a grand success not only bringing unprecedented prosperity to the farmer but also boosting the country's total food production. The *China Daily* reported in 1984 that, for the first time in her history, China became a major exporter of grain.[2]

I went again to the church on Sunday. The senior pastor's wife, Mrs. Hsu Yao Kwuan, again met me at the gates of the compound.

"Since you were here last, we have started a seminary," she said and took me to see the new sixty-thousand-dollar, two-story classroom and office building. "We have a faculty of eight professors teaching courses in Old Testament, New Testament, logic and philosophy, church and secular history, geography (including biblical), English, and Chinese languages."

As I met the students, she said, "There are forty-seven students enrolled from the provinces. Fifteen are women. They come to study for two years here and then they will go back as ministers to their home communities."

Another church was to open soon in Chengdu. Thirty-five churches were then open throughout the province. There has been a revival of Christianity in Sichuan.

I was told that many house churches met openly and freely to read the

Bible, sing, and pray. The church Hsu pastors also conducts weekday Bible studies on Wednesdays and Thursdays.

As we gathered for the worship service, again the sanctuary was packed. Chairs were set in the courtyard, where a second congregation listened over a public address system. The godly pastor, Hsu, now past eighty, was still vigorous. He preached a marvelous sermon on "Mary, who chose the better part by sitting at the feet of Jesus."

As we sang the closing hymn "Jesus, Keep Me Near the Cross," I looked up again at the banner above the pulpit, the white cross on the field of red velvet. I choked up and could not sing. I had come back again to the family of faith in Chengdu, but not all the family was present in the flesh. Wallace Wang had died.

The white cross seemed to be a white handkerchief. Wallace Wang was waving it, saying, "I will see you again . . . in heaven."

Above the banner of the cross the single word, *Hallelujah,* was still there!

Notes

1. Richard B. Thomas, "A Letter from the Publisher," *Time* magazine, January 6, 1986, p. 4.

2. "China Plans to Raise Output of Grain to Record in 1986," *Herald Tribune,* International Edition, Beijing (Reuter) China, January 6, 1986.

"Resurrection Day" in China at the Dongshan Church in Guangzhou (Canton). 2000 people packed the church on the first Easter after the church was reopened in 1979.

Author and the pastors of the Chengdu Church two months after reopening in 1980. Senior Pastor Hsu Dao Kwuan is third from right and Mrs. Hsu at the extreme left.

Penglai Church (in NE China) where missionary Lottie Moon attended. Like all churches, it was closed during the cultural revolution and converted to other uses.

The Great Wall of China, a section near Beijing. Construction began two centuries before Christ and ultimately extended 3500 miles across China.

The Li River in Southwest China and the fabled and spectacular mountain scenery.

A member of Beijing's Chongwenmen Church proudly displays his new Bible. The Chinese have published and distributed over 2 million Bibles in the past decade. A new Bible press has been installed in Nanjing with a capacity to print over one million Bibles a year and other Christian literature.

Many churches in China are packed and overflowing. Here a second congregation is seated in the courtyard, listening to the service over a public address system. Sichuan Province, 1985.

Deacons meeting at the church in Guilin. Two men and two women meet with the pastor and share the universal common concerns of a local church—evangelism, finances, and pastoral needs of the congregation.

One of the six pastors of the Grace Church of Shanghai leads the Tuesday night Bible study. By means of a flip chart the congregation is learning a new hymn, our familiar gospel song, "Lord, I'm Coming Home."

A kindergarten class in Shanghai poses for a picture. Schools provide a full daycare program since both parents usually have full-time jobs.

Fisherman with his "snake birds," trained cormorants that dive for fish, pursuing their quarry to depths of 50 feet.

Seminary students work to pay their way in seminary. These two are cooking soup in the kitchen at the Guangzhou (Canton) Seminary.

Beijing Pastor Yin Chi Chen with members of his family, "four generations of Christians." During the Cultural Revolution, the Christian faith was kept alive within the family in private secret house churches.

6

The Coming of the Dawn
Xi'an (Sian)

When and how did Christianity first enter China? This dramatic chapter in the history of Christian missions lay buried, lost, and unknown for centuries. And when discovered, it told the story of a missionary of whom the modern world had never heard and of a Chinese Christian community that had flourished over a thousand years ago.

The Mysterious Tablet

The saga begins in AD 1625 at a village in north central China called Chouchih. Workmen, digging a foundation for a building, unearthed a large black limestone tablet covered with inscriptions. These were Chinese characters and other writing in a strange script.

The mysterious tablet created quite a sensation. The governor of the province came to examine it. His scholars recognized the fine calligraphy from a very ancient period. But they could not understand the strange Chinese words or identify the foreign language. The governor ordered the monument taken to a Taoist temple thirty miles away in Changan (the county seat). There it was mounted on a pedestal under an ornate canopy for all the city to see.

The tablet was the object of endless speculation and pious veneration. What was the subject matter of the text? Who wrote it? How old was it?

Chang Kang-yu, a scholar for the royal court, made a rubbing of the inscription and sent it to a friend, Dr. Leo Li, in Hangzhou (Hangchow). When Dr. Li, with the help of Jesuit missionaries, deciphered and published the text, the story it told spread like wildfire not only in China but throughout the Western world.

The tablet, inscribed in beautiful, classical, ninth-century calligraphy, carried the date of the second year of the great T'ang (AD 781). It told the story of the first Christian missionary to China who had come 150 years earlier.

The place where the light of the gospel first shone in the darkness of China was the great city of Changan (near present-day Xi'an, which means "eternal peace"), at that time the largest city in the world with a million population. Changan was the cultural center of ancient China and a paradigm of imperial splendor. Called Golden Cathay by Westerners, it was easily the richest city in the world, and its grandeur and exotic life-style were legendary.

Changan was near the beginning of the Silk Road which ran westward between the mighty massifs of the Tibetan Mountains and the Himalayas. From there the road continued to the Golden Gates of Samarkand, to Bagdad and to the Mediterranean ports of Tyre and Antioch. Down this road traveled the caravans transporting jade, spices, and bales of silk (China's closely guarded secret) bound for the markets of Asia and Europe. Armies, ambassadors, diplomats, traders, and travelers moved along the Silk Road to all the principalities of Central Asia. It was the golden age of the T'ang Dynasty, a time of openness, trade, and great prosperity. Down this road had come Alopen, a Persian Nestorian Christian missionary, from the region of present-day Syria. He arrived in Changan in AD 635.

The emperor, T'ai Tsung, had inherited the empire by killing his older and younger brothers (who were conspiring to kill him). Though begun in violence, T'ai's reign was wise and benevolent. It is recorded that upon his ascending the throne, his first act was to dismiss three thousand concubines from the imperial palace. He established a library of two hundred thousand books. He received the Nestorian missionary with pomp and ceremony.

An account of the next 150 years is detailed on what is now called the Nestorian Tablet.

The "Luminous Doctrine"

The tablet is entitled "A Monument To The Diffusion Through the

Middle Kingdom Of The Illustrious Teachings of Ta Ch'in (Alopen of Syria)." It summarizes the Christian faith, expressed in distinctive Chinese terms. A significant omission is any reference to the crucifixion and the resurrection. Then follows a brief account of the apostolic age.

It tells of Alopen, a man of high virtue, arriving in the court of the great T'ai Tsung and of the emperor's proclamation commending the doctrine of Alopen. It records that the emperor had looked with favor on the writings Alopen brought (the Bible) and the "Luminous Doctrine" (Christianity) that he taught. The emperor instructed that a monastery be built in Changan and twenty other monasteries constructed throughout the country for the teaching of this new religion. Finally, the inscription describes the spread of Christianity throughout the kingdom, the building of churches, and the struggles with Buddhist opposition for the next 150 years.

After such an auspicious beginning, what happened? Within another century, the pendulum of popular support began to swing back. A new dynasty took the throne. Military reverses on China's western border created an atmosphere of suspicion of all things foreign. The Taoist monks increased in power and favor with the royal court. Christianity was suppressed, and the Nestorian Christian community in China disappeared.

The fruit of the labors of Alopen, the Nestorian Christian, and his colleagues that flourished for a century and a half were completely obliterated. Not a single artifact of the Christian era has been found. There is no record in Chinese history, literature, or legend of this earliest Christian community or of Alopen, the first missionary, other than this single account of the Nestorian Tablet. The Luminous Doctrine that shined so brightly in the darkness had disappeared in China.

The Nestorians

Who were these Nestorian Christians whose envoy, Alopen, first took the gospel to China?

The name comes from Nestorius, a theologian and church leader who died in AD 451. He was condemned as a heretic by the Roman Church for teaching that Christ was two persons, one divine and the other human. The orthodox doctrine of the incarnation was that Christ was a single person, at once God and man.

Nestorius's followers were concentrated in the region of Persia (present-day Syria, Iraq, and Iran). They built many churches and were extremely missionary-minded. Because they were Oriental in mind, culture, and dress, the Nestorians were very effective in evangelizing parts of Egypt, India, central Asia, and, through Alopen, China. For five hundred years the Nestorian churches were a strong and dominant Christian force in the Middle East and Asia.

Several factors seem to have been responsible for the demise of the Nestorian churches. First, the churches became worldly, apostate from biblical doctrine. The Nestorian Church also became political, losing its impact on the culture. Finally Muslim persecutions and war decimated them.

In the end, the Nestorians were all but completely wiped out by Tamerlane, the cruelest and most ruthless of all medieval conquerors, during a period of slaughter and devastation that lasted from 1358 to 1405. The few Nestorian Christians who survived fled into the mountain valleys of Kurdistan. They are known today as the Assyrian Church, with a constituency of about one hundred thousand, most of whom live in Iran and Iraq.

The Second Wave

After Alopen's mission, Nestorian Christians penetrated China a second time.

Marco Polo and his Franciscan contemporaries reported the presence of Nestorian Christian groups in China in the thirteenth century. One traveler calculated there were more than thirty thousand Nestorians worshiping in impressive churches. But he noted that they appeared to be foreigners, not Chinese. A Franciscan missionary observed that the Chinese priests were "most ignorant" of theology and the gospel.

Ancient Christian manuscripts discovered in caves in Gansu Province northwest of Xi'an confirm the existence of this later Nestorian Christian community in China. Were these Chinese Christians the fruit of Alopen's missionary work from seed that had lain dormant for centuries? Recent discoveries indicate that this was an entirely separate and independent new wave of Nestorian Christians who entered China five centuries after Alopen.

The northern and western boundaries of China were ringed by nomadic Turkish, Mongol, and Tatar tribes from Central Asia. Nestorian missionaries evangelized many of these nomadic peoples and whole tribes like the Naimans and the Keraits became Christian. Many of the warlike Uygurs were also converted.

The Western world already knew of Christians among these nomadic tribes of Central Asia. There were strange stories about a legendary Christian ruler of the East who called himself "Prester John." He was a Nestorian Christian, a Karakita chieftan, Gur Khan, who was said to be a lineal descendant of the Magi who had visited the Christ child.

Then came the great Mongol explosion out of Central Asia led by the fearsome Genghis Khan. Genghis Khan's army swept to the East and took the imperial throne of China. These nomadic, warlike tribes from Central Asia, with their huge populations, inevitably followed him. The Uygurs, Naimans, Keraits, and others settled throughout northern China. Some of these were Nestorian Christians who brought their faith with them.

The *Zanmei Shi (New China Hymnal)* recently published by the China Christian Council carries a newly discovered hymn from the Nestorian period. The seven-hundred-year-old hymn is a song of praise to the loving Father God declaring:

> The highest heavens with deep reverence adore,
> All the people learn the joys of God's peace.
> Great God of all gives an inner peace to all,
> He is our everpresent loving Father God.[1]

We now know that this second colony of Nestorian Christians reported by Marco Polo were not indigenous Chinese believers descended from the followers of Alopen. They were non-Chinese immigrants from Central Asia. This Christian witness also eventually died out, although the tribal peoples remained scattered across the northern part of China, and today are almost entirely Muslim in faith.

A Soft Seat to Xi'an

Instead of first and second class, train travel in China is designated "soft seat" or "hard seat." I took an eighteen-hour soft seat sleeper train ride from Chengdu to see Xi'an, Alopen's city where, in the remote and distant past, the gospel had twice florished and died.

The Pullman was an older European design with closed compartments accommodating four people. In the daytime, passengers sat on the lower bunks, facing each other. At bedtime, two climbed into the uppers to sleep. There was no ladder, only a footrest on the wall. Nor were there any curtains. Passengers accepted whoever was assigned to the compartment, male or female, old or young. They slept in their clothes or nonchalantly changed on their bunks. It was no place for the modest.

Meals, served in an antique dining car, were simple. The one lavatory at the end of the car was Spartan, containing a mirror, a washbasin, and a metal commode that looked straight down at the track flying by below.

In spite of the lack of amenities, the train ride across the heartland of China is a memorable highlight that I heartily recommend.

The route lay north and east, across Sichuan and Shaanxi Provinces. We were traveling a valley cut by the Chia-ling Chiang, another of the four tributaries of the mighty Yangtze River. We were soon in precipitous mountains, slowly negotiating curves and switchbacks where we could look down and see the caboose trailing in the opposite direction. Mountain streams and cascading waterfalls laced dense emerald forests like silky white ribbons.

The Seedbed of Communism

Once over the Chia-ling mountain range, we were in a China different from the lush Chengdu basin. This was Shaanxi Province, one of the poorest and most backward in all China.

When the missionary Alopen arrived in China during the golden era of the T'ang Dynasty, this was a rich, fertile, and productive area. The hillsides were covered with heavy vegetation. The valleys were watered with a vast and efficient irrigation system that fed a half-million acres.

But centuries of human occupation and abuse of the land turned the verdant garden into a semidesert. Every year the farmers set fire to the mountains, burning off the vegetation, so the spring rains could wash down the topsoil to enrich the valley. In time the mountains were denuded, eroded, and gullied. The irrigation systems became clogged with silt and were neglected. To further compound the destruction, the hardpan surface of the barren mountains and the deeply eroded ravines funneled the spring rains into the valley in torrential floods.

The deteriorating ecology of Shaanxi was further hastened by continuing cycles of devastating droughts. The province adjoins the empty vastness of Inner Mongolia to the north, where lie the desolate Gobi and Ordos deserts. Searing winds out of the desert drive stifling clouds of dry heat and gritty dust over Shaanxi.

In addition to calamitous natural disasters, the people of Shaanxi have been ravaged by two civil wars in this century alone.

A thousand years of impoverishment by flood and drought and declining fertility and productivity plunged the Shaanxi peasant into crushing poverty. At times whole counties were depopulated by these apocalyptic scourges.

The peasants also suffered at the hands of feudal warlords and oppressive governments. In the past, less than 10 percent of the population owned more than 80 percent of the land. Rent, crop shares, taxes, graft, and usury literally enslaved the poor peasants. Children of a poor family could be seized in payment of a debt, although a teenage girl in a poor crop year was not worth a bushel of grain.[2] As a common practice, newborn infants were drowned because the family could not endure feeding another mouth.

The endemic poverty and dire distress of the Shaanxi farmers became fertile soil for the seed of dissent and revolution. In the 1920s Shaanxi was the chief port of entry for Communist ideology reaching China from the Soviet Union to the north.

Mao capitalized on the bitterness and discontent of the Chinese peasants who comprised 80 percent of the population. Mao built a peasant army in his revolution (in contrast to the Russian revolution that mobilized the urban factory workers). The peasants were tough, hardened from childhood by physical labor. They were accustomed to deprivations. After centuries of bondage in medieval serfdom, they owned no property and had no stake in the existing system. They fought with total abandon and made superb, invincible guerrilla fighters.

Here in this seedbed of bitter poverty and hopeless discontent, the Communists created the first all-Socialist society in China in the city of Yan'an in northwest Shaanxi. Yan'an was the Communist Revolutionary Army's military base from which Mao's forces began the victorious march southward.

The new People's Republic of China immediately came to grips with the plight of the peasants with remarkable success. In the short span of thirty-five years, the Chinese government accomplished many changes.

—Rural China is organized into a unified political structure for the first time in modern history.

—Security and improved public health is provided in the rural villages where, in most cases, it had been practically nonexistent.

—China's grain output has doubled through increased irrigation, better seed, and new chemical fertilizers, allowing her to not only feed her people but to export the surplus.

—The "four pests"—rats, grain-eating sparrows, mosquitoes, and flies—have been virtually eliminated. (Today visitors are amazed to find no flies in China!)

—The life expectancy of the average peasant has tripled. Before 1949 when famine, pestilence, wars, and banditry wracked the rural area, life expectancy was only twenty to twenty-five years. Now the average peasant's life expectancy is sixty-four years. This is a far better record than other developing nations, such as India and Brazil.

As our train came out of the mountains into the low-lying hills and valleys, I began to see the evidence of Shaanxi's prosperity: square brick houses with red tile roofs, brick and pottery minifactories, herds of holstein dairy cattle, sleek yellow draft oxen, horses, mules, and red tractors working the fields.

In the irrigated valleys, the checkerboard fields were abundant with leeks, cabbage, tobacco, corn, oats, and cotton. Groves of fruit trees—apples, pears, and apricots—dotted the landscape. Rows of stately, thin poplars lined the roads and farm paths.

City of Eternal Peace

Shaanxi's present agricultural glory is not paralleled by urban glory. An example is the once-proud city of Changan now called Xi'an. By the middle of the twentieth century, the golden city of the illustrious T'angs, the great capital of the empire of China, the largest and most magnificent city in the world, was reduced to a squalid and backward settlement in the hinterland with a population one-sixth its former size.

Until 1974 Xi'an was remote, relatively unknown and of little interest to anyone outside China. Then the city captured the world's attention with the most amazing archeological discovery of the century, the astonishing burial site of Emperor Qin Shi Huangdi and thousands of life-size terra-cotta horses and soldiers. Almost overnight Xi'an became a popular tourist destination for Chinese and foreigners, rivaling Beijing and Shanghai.

Our train arrived in Xi'an exactly on time. Met by our guide, an exuberant college student named Mr. Ho, we were hustled to the Xi'an Guest House, a new modern fourteen-story facility with many conveniences, a bank, post office, and a variety of quality shops. It was a splendid location with a magnificent view of the ancient walled city to the north and immediately facing the picturesque Small Wild Goose Pagoda.

At lunch in a downtown restaurant, we felt the boom-town dynamics of Xi'an with its two-and-a-half million people. The sidewalks were jammed with people. The bustling, hurrying mass spilled onto the streets and choked the crosswalks at the traffic lights. Peddlers were everywhere selling ice cream, cold drinks, baskets, hemp bags, and embroidered red jackets. Tiny sidewalk booths offered noodles, tea, chopped chicken, and fried pork.

On tour we drove through the western gate of the massive stone walls that enclose the city in a perfect square. Ho said, "Six hundred years old . . . Ming dynasty . . . . On the foundation of the ancient wall of two thousand years ago . . . thirty-six feet high, thirty feet wide at the top." The huge, buttressed battlements and broad moat are an impressive example of an ancient fortified Chinese city very similar to that which Alopen must have seen fifteen centuries ago.

Six miles east of Xi'an on a bluff on the Chan River is the Banpo Museum. Here in 1953 workmen digging in the ground accidentally discovered a Neolithic village at least eight thousand years old. Traces of a village of one hundred houses, Stone Age pottery, tools, and human bones were uncovered.

This would indicate that Chinese communal life and urban culture probably had its beginnings in the Wei Ho Valley as early as 6,000 BC. This also confirms that the Chinese are indigenous to the land they still occupy.

The location of the village of Banpo also indicates that what developed later as the Silk Road was, from antiquity, an important route for the movement of primitive peoples.

The Trader's Son

Mr. Ho told us a story.

A farmer and a trader were talking. The trader asked the farmer, "How much profit do you make farming?"

"Ten percent," the farmer said.

"A trader makes 100 percent," the trader said and then asked, "What makes a warlord?"

"Money," answered the farmer.

"I will make the money and make you a warlord," the trader promised. So it happened.

One day the trader brought a beautiful girl to the warlord to be his concubine. The warlord discovered the girl was pregnant by the trader. He killed the trader but claimed as his son the boy who was born.

Mr. Ho said, "That is the story of how Qin Shi Huangdi, son of a trader and adopted son of a farmer-warlord, himself became a warlord at thirteen years of age."

Qin, through twenty-five years of ruthless battles, conquered his rival warlords "like a silkworm devouring a mulberry leaf." By 212 BC Qin had unified China into one true nation for the first time in her history.

Qin established the concept of royalty, naming himself the first emperor, developed a feudal structure of society, and declared Changan (Xi'an) the first capital of a united China.

The imperial city that Qin built was by far the largest, wealthiest, and most magnificent city in the world in its day. Its fortified, stone-walled perimeter measured six miles on each side and housed a quarter of a million people and temples, 270 elaborate palaces, and many gardens. Obsessed with security, Qin changed his sleeping quarters every night. Anyone who revealed the emperor's whereabouts was put to death with his whole family.

To consolidate his power, Qin transported 120,000 wealthy families from all parts of the empire to live in Changan, enfeebling the feudal aristocracy by removing them from the land and people who gave them power.

The emperor was a ruthless tyrant. He burned all the books of Confucius and buried 460 scholars in the ground up to their necks and then chopped off their heads.

Although Qin was a cruel and harsh emperor, he was a practical and successful monarch. He codified the laws and standarized weights and measures. He built a vast network of roads radiating from the capital and standarized axle lengths of wagons and chariots to enable vehicles to travel in the same ruts. He built the Grand Canal, the greatest inland water communication system in the ancient world, which is still in use today. He introduced an irrigation system that claimed vast wastelands for agriculture and is functioning today.

Qin began the building of the Great Wall of China across the north to keep the marauding Mongol tribesmen out. Thousands, perhaps millions, of workmen perished in its construction. The wall has been given the grim title of "the longest cemetery in the world."

When Qin assumed the throne at age thirteen, he immediately began the construction of his own mausoleum. What he accomplished in lavish splendor and architectural grandeur far exceeds anything else in the world, including the pyramids, tombs, and monuments of the Egyptian pharaohs. Qin's mausoleum was built by thousands of workmen over thirty-six years.

What Qin actually built was a magnificent city, reputedly adorned with streams of mercury, houses of gold, and vaults filled with imperial treasures. Then the whole city was buried under a mountain of dirt fifteen stories high, leaving a tunneled access into the emperor's tomb.

When Qin died, he was buried in his underground Palace of Death. The new emperor ordered the great jade door of the tomb sealed and the royal pallbearers, court officials, eunuchs, and craftsmen buried alive with him. The shaft was plugged with dirt, and Qin was sealed in his subterranean palace.

"This is Mount Li, the Emperor Qin Shi Huangdi's tomb," Mr. Ho said, as we stood before the giant earthen mountain. Two stone stelae stand at the entrance of a pathway leading to the summit where fields of wheat and pomegranate trees now grow. "China lacks the money and a sufficient number of trained archaeologists to excavate the whole tomb. Besides, helping the living is more important to China than studying the dead."

The Xi'an Soldiers

Three quarters of a mile beyond Qin's tomb, or Tumulus as the mountain is called, we came to the site where a peasant, who was digging an irrigation well, found some pieces of terra-cotta that appeared to be very old. Authorities examined the artifacts in 1974 and began seven years of excavations that eventually uncovered a virtual army of terra-cotta soldiers and horses guarding the main approach to Emperor Qin's tomb.

The site is now covered with a hangar-like building two and one-half times the length of a football field and twice as wide. In an excavated three and one-half acre pit, sixteen feet deep, the terra-cotta soldiers with their war chariots and horses stand in battle formation, rank on rank, as if only awaiting an order to charge into action. Seventy archers with their crossbows are at the front. Behind them, at attention, stand soldiers with bronze spears and swords. Soldiers on the flanks face outward, while kneeling archers are poised for attack.

The terra-cotta figures were molded out of clay and then fired. The torsos are hollow; the legs and arms, solid. Every soldier is a unique work of art. Each face was individually crafted and different, modeled from among the many racial groups in Qin's living army. There is a variety of uniforms and variations in clothing.

The soldiers stand six feet tall (or more), larger than the average Chinese. The royal guards were probably selected from the populace because of their size and were better fed than the average Chinese.

The horses stand four abreast, hitched to the royal war chariots with leather harness and brass fittings. Their ears are set forward, tense and alert, with forelocks curled and tails knotted.

The horses in the excavation are not short-legged Chinese ponies, but the "celestial" horses of the emperors. These leggy animals were from the Fergana Valley in Central Asia. The emperors sent expeditions to seize the horses from their owners and bring them back as breeding stock. They were swift, sinewy steeds with great stamina and considered celestial or heavenly because of a special peculiarity of "sweating blood." This phenomenon was unexplained until recently when it was discovered that a burrowing parasite peculiar to that area attacked the capillaries until they bled.

"It will take one to two centuries to excavate fully the royal burial complex," said Chinese archeologist Uan Zhongyi. Only one pit has been excavated, and it took twelve years to do that. There are between three hundred and four hundred identifiable pits similar to the one excavated, containing thousands of terra-cotta statuary and other artifacts. The burial complex itself is twenty miles square. The royal tomb is at the center. A half-life-size bronze chariot pulled by four celestial horses was among the treasures discovered in the excavations.

Out by the gates, we found an enterprising Chinese man with a crude reproduction of the imperial chariot hitched to a horse. He was hawking rides and a photo for one yuan (about thirty cents U.S.).

Ali! Ali!

"Young people are not interested in religion. We are scientific," Mr. Ho explained as we visited Xi'an's Great Mosque, one of the largest in China. A long-robed caretaker told us it was founded in AD 742 during the T'ang Dynasty. He said, "On the Muslim New Year, the mosque and the four courtyards are filled with people."

In 1985 the most famous Muslim in the world, former world boxing champion Muhammad Ali joined Chinese Muslims for prayer in the 1,200-year-old mosque. The imam, Ma Liangji, told the congregation that Ali had "won fame for Muslims the world over and Chinese Muslims take pride in his achievements." The caretaker was quite impressed when I told him that Ali was from my hometown, Louisville, and I knew him as Cassius Clay!

The Muslim religion came into China from the West by way of the Silk Road, as did Christianity. Alopen entered Xi'an three years after the prophet Muhammad died. Islam entered Xi'an during the golden years of the T'ang Dynasty and built the first mosque just one hundred years after the first Nestorian churches were built.

The Muslim faith, with its strict monotheism, abhorrence of idolatry, prescribed worship, and hope to gain paradise by good deeds, was appealing to the Chinese. Today there are more than fifteen hundred functioning mosques in northwestern China and an estimated twenty million Muslims.

Because the government recognized the Muslim Chinese primarily as a minority people rather than a religious group, they have not experienced antireligious oppression in the past to the same degree as Christianity and Buddhism. They have been given official protection to practice their customs in religion, and their special dietary restrictions are respected.

Muslims, wherever found, have been one of the most difficult peoples in the world to reach with the gospel. Before 1949 Swedish missionaries and the China Inland Mission had limited work among the Muslim minorities, especially the Uygurs. A church of converted Muslims was established in Kashgar in the far west on the border between China and Russia. But in the late 1930s a wave of Muslim persecution scattered the Christians, and many believers were martyred.

Britt Towery told me of a recent visit in the heart of Muslim China, to Urumqi (formerly Turkestan), the capital of Xinjiang Province. He visited a Christian church where the auditorium was packed and one hundred people were in another room listening over a public address system. There are six thousand Christians in this Gobi desert city in fifteen house churches scattered over the area. However, all these believers are Han Chinese. No one knew of any Uygurs who had been converted to Christianity. "Both in face and faith they are distinctly Muslim-Arab," Towery said.

The Legend of the Wild Goose

"Many years ago in India, a band of starving Buddhist monks were kneeling and praying for food. When a flock of geese flying overhead saw their plight, the leader heard their prayer, broke his wing, and fell into their midst. Moved by the sacrifice, the monks buried the goose instead of eating it and built a temple on the site in memory of the goose." Thus Mr. Ho explained the origin of the name Big Wild Goose Pagoda.

When Xuan Zang, the monk who introduced Buddhism to China, returned from India after an eighteen-year pilgrimage, he brought the Sutras, the sacred writing of Buddhism, to Xi'an. The Crown Prince Li Zhi, in memory of his mother, built the Big Wild Goose Pagoda where the monks could translate the sacred books from the Sanskrit into Chinese. That was in AD 652, just seven years after the Chinese missionary Alopen had come to Xi'an.

The Big Wild Goose Pagoda is an impressive seven-story monument that towers 210 feet over the countryside. It is designated as a national monument and, in 1984 under the government's policy of freedom of worship, was completely restored and returned to the Buddhist monks. When we visited several monks were around the altar, occasionally striking a five-foot gong and gladly posing for pictures. The pagoda was packed with Chinese sightseers who were just as curious as we were, snapping pictures and buying souvenirs. Only an occasional worshiper came from the milling crowd to kneel at the altar and place a lighted taper before the gilded Buddha.

The Forest of Stelae

The Shaanxi Provincial Museum, a former Confucian temple, contains a rich collection of more than four thousand separate exhibits that tell the story of China from its earliest beginnings.

One exhibit, the "Forest of Stelae," is a collection of 1,095 stone tablets gathered from all over China. The stelae are the history books of China, recording the events, people, philosophy, and epics of the past. The stones are carved in a wide variety of calligraphy, from primitive to classical.

While looking for the Nestorian stelae, Mr. Ho told me an interesting story.

"When the stone was discovered, a wealthy Englishman bought it for a large sum of money. The stelae were delivered to London and placed in the British Museum. However, the Chinese official had outsmarted the foreigner. He had an exact copy made of the stela and shipped the duplicate to England. the original is still here in Xi'an."

When I saw the Nestorian stela, I was utterly amazed. I had expected something like a plaque or cornerstone. It is a monument of polished black oolitic limestone, nine feet tall, three and one-half feet across, a foot thick. At the top of the stela is a carving of two dragons holding a pearl. The dragon is China; the pearl of great price is the gospel.

Inscribed on the next line is a cross surmounting a lotus blossom and a cloud. Again, the symbolism is clear. The cross is over the lotus (a Buddhist symbol) and also over the cloud (a Taoist and Muslim symbol). Then, line upon line, the massive script of the stela tells the story of Alopen's bringing Christianity to China. It is recorded that the Emperor T'ai Tsung bestowed on Alopen the title of "Bishop of the Great Law, by which law he governs a kingdom of China in great peace, and the church filled the whole country with the prosperity of preaching." This was the record of the dawning of Christianity in China! But it was a false dawn, breaking dimly for about 150 years. Then China plunged into darkness again.

Again in 1269 the emperor, Kublai Khan, sent a letter to the pope by Maffeo and Nicolo Polo (the uncle and father of Marco), asking him for one hundred men "wise in the Christian law and acquainted with the seven arts" to bring Christianity to the Chinese people. Instead of one hundred, only two Dominican friars were sent along with letters for Kublai Khan. The two missionaries set out with the Polos for China, but the terrors of the East discouraged them and they turned back. Marco

Polo and his party continued the journey alone. They were warmly received in the court of the great Kublai Khan in 1275 and sadly reported that they had brought no Christian teachers with them.[3]

Again, it was a false dawn, and centuries of darkness followed.

Before leaving Xi'an, I was told that a Christian church had been reopened on Easter a few months before. The church was packed with believers, and there was great rejoicing, singing, and weeping.

We left our hotel early in the morning for a flight to Beijing. As we drove through the city on the way to the airport, I thought of the tiny Christian congregation that was hidden somewhere in the dark maze of streets and houses. That tiny band of Christians was a light shining in a sea of darkness. As we were airborne, the sun was rising in the east.

I asked myself, *Is this the breaking of a new dawn over China?* Then I remembered what the Chinese religious leader Han Wenzao had said to me only a few months earlier: "Christianity came to China at four distinct times in history. It came first in the seventh century with the Nestorians, who disappeared entirely. Then again the Nestorians came in the thirteenth century and disappeared. The Catholics came in the sixteenth century and they practically disappeared. Finally, the Protestants and Catholics came in the nineteenth century and Christianity has thus far survived. But in every movement Christianity had the image of a foreign importation. Now we must learn from history. It is important for the Chinese Christians to have our church deeply rooted in the soil of China, an indigenous Chinese church. That is the entire purpose of the Three-Self Movement: Self-support, Self-control, Self-propagation for the church."[4]

In the early morning light I looked back at Xi'an, and somewhere in the darkness was the tiny Three-Self Christian Church. I looked again toward the pastel sky of the rising sun and said to myself, *The true dawn is breaking over China.*

Notes

1. Britt Towery, trans., "The Highest Heavens Adore," *The New China Hymnal, Zanmei Shi* (Nanjing Press: China Christian Council, 1985).

2. Ding Chen, "The Economic Development of China," *Scientific American,* September 1980, p. 152.

3. Columbo Cary-Elwes, *China and the Cross* (New York: P. O. Kenedy and Sons, 1956), p. 48.

4. Personal interview with Han Wenzao, general secretary of Amity Foundation, Nanjing, China.

7

Where the Giant Stood Up

Beijing (Peking)

On a wintry day in October 1949, Mao Zedong, heavily bundled up against the north wind, stood on the rostrum atop Beijing's Gate of Heavenly Peace.

To his back was the mysterious Forbidden City where the emperors and their wives. concubines, retinues, and Pekingese dogs had lived for centuries in royal isolation from the people. In front of him was an enormous crowd of thousands—students, peasants, factory workers, and soldiers—massed in the vast Tian'anmen Square.

"The Chinese people have stood up," Mao shouted to the thundering crowd as he raised the flag of the People's Republic of China and launched a new era in the history of an ancient people.

The long, brutal, and debilitating civil war was over. The endless chain of feudal bondage had been broken. The exploitation of China by foreign powers was ended. Mao took a prostrate China by the hand, lifted her up, and promised her dignity, pride, identity, and self-determination.

Twenty-nine years later, in the summer of 1978, I was standing at this historic site in Tian'anmen Square where the new China was cradled.

"Chairman Mao spoke from right there," Ms. Shih Chinhsia (a university student who was our Beijing guide) said, pointing to the majestic, sunbathed, temple-style Gate of Heavenly Peace. A billboard-size portrait of the great liberator hung over the main portal, flanked by giant banners on each side declaring, "Long live the Chinese People's Republic" and "Long live the great solidarity of the people of the world."

During the Cultural Revolution, Shih was sent to Mongolia as a goatherder to "share the revolutionary experience." After four years of common labor, she had been allowed to resume her education.

Ms. Shih was fluent in English. She was quiet, serious, and plain. Her long black hair was pulled tightly off her face and hung in two braids. She wore a white cotton blouse, blue peasant trousers, and sandals.

"Tien'anmen is the largest public square in the world," Ms. Shih proudly declared, "holding two million people and measuring forty hectares." I calculated mentally: one hundred acres, or the length of six football fields on each side!

On the east side of the square is the huge Revolutionary Museum. On the west is the quarter-mile-long Great Hall of the People, where the People's Congress for the Communist Party meets. In this hall in 1972 Zhou Enlai entertained President Nixon and five thousand dinner guests.

The Faltering Giant

"Leave everything on the bus and follow me," Ms. Shih instructed. "Tourists may go to the head of the line." She led us past a line of thousands of people, four abreast, snaking the full length of the square, and waiting to enter a golden-yellow-tiled building with red granite columns.

At the steps, the Chinese politely moved aside; we silently and somberly filed into the foyer. A larger-than-life, white marble statue of Chairman Mao greeted us. He was seated in an upholstered chair set against a magnificent landscape backdrop, a velvet tapestry entitled "Mountains and Rivers of the Motherland."

The line parted in front of the statue, passing by twos around the tapestry and joining again on the other side.

There in a crystal sarcophagus reclined the body of Chairman Mao, as though in peaceful sleep. White-robed attendants stood near with wheelchairs and stretchers. Peasants, workers, and soldiers filed by. Many were weeping and groaning, visibly shaken. Mao had been dead only eighteen months. The people's great leader for twenty-seven years was gone. One person broke into restrained hysteria and fainted. The white-robed attendants moved quickly to carry him out.

As I watched the endless column of mourners pass the flag-draped casket, I felt the immensity of their depression. Mao's widow and self-chosen heir was in a Shanghai prison, a part of the notorious Gang of Four. In the revolving door of Chinese Communist Party politics, Deng Xioaping had emerged as the leader of the pack. But he was the same age as Mao and a two-time loser in previous power struggles. Deng was surrounded by rivals in the old palace guard and ambitious radicals in the ranks, all jockeying for power. China, the standing giant, was faltering in the throes of deep grief and uncertainty.

Outside the mausoleum in Tien'anmen Square I mixed with the crowd. Some of the people were friendly and curious; others, timidly cautious and subdued. I watched the thousand of bicycles flowing like a river down the broad avenue, everyone starting, stopping, and pedaling at exactly the same slow speed. No one cut out of line or sped ahead. This was Mao's China, millions of people blended into a symmetrical pattern by three decades of rigid discipline, enforced uniformity, and the suppression of individualism for the sake of the collective whole. Mao forged the strongest central government in China's history and anchored the power of that government in the capital, Beijing.

The discovery of the fossil remains of Peking man near Beijing indicates that early man existed here a half-million years ago. In early Chinese history, the settlement on the treeless, marshy banks of the river was called Kitaia, from which the name *Cathay* came.

The Mongol, Kublai Khan (1215-1294), first established what is now present-day Beijing as the capital of the Chinese Empire. Kublai Khan designed and laid out the city much as it is today. Marco Polo visited here in 1275. At its cultural peak in the Ming Dynasty, Beijing had 780 palaces, pavilions, and temples.

The Forbidden City

"In the feudal period, common people who entered the Forbidden City were immediately put to death," Ms. Shih told us as we walked through the imposing bloodred Gate of Heavenly Peace. "Now, the Imperial Palace is open to everyone." As we stepped into a broad courtyard, white marble bridges, gold-tiled roofs, columned pavilions, and royal red palaces glistened in the Beijing sun in an endless display of dazzling splendor.

The Imperial City covers 250 acres and is encircled by a massive stone wall 35 feet high and a moat 130 feet wide. There are five main palaces and 9,000 rooms where a succession of 24 royal "sons of heaven" have lived.

In the Forbidden City we visited a seemingly endless number of imposing columned palaces that carried such poetic names as Heavenly Purity, Earthly Tranquillity, Literary Splendor, Preserving Harmony, and Military Eminence. Rooms were filled with art treasures of gold, jade, and precious stones. Everywhere were fierce stone lions, copper caldrons, bronze tortoises, dragon gargoyles and gilded gates festooned with carvings.

This distinctive Chinese architecture, developed over the millennia, influenced building design throughout Asia. Unlike Western construction that developed in Europe, the roofs of Chinese buildings were supported by columns rather than walls. This necessitated a complex bracketing system known as *duo gong*. This system of concave roofs, columns, and bracketed beams created the venerable architecture that is another of China's inventive contributions to the the reservoir of world culture.

Beijing is repository of imperial monuments and interesting activities. During the next two days, we walked the 692-acre Summer Palace (a repeat of the architecture and opulence of the Imperial City) and were reminded that the palace was twice burned and looted by Western imperialist troops. Many of China's art treasures are now in the museums of Paris, London, and Taipei. We attended a Chinese opera in an open-air park, understanding neither the words nor music but utterly fascinated by the elaborate costumes and exaggerated acting. The daring and breathtaking performance of the famous Chinese acrobats caused us to gasp. We shopped at the official government Friendship Store where a banner declared in English, "We have friends all over the world." The Children's Palace, a former imperial garden, is now a school for five thousand especially gifted children. After visiting a jade and ivory carving factory, cloisonne shop, silk painting studio, embroidery factory, Buddhist monastery, and Taoist temple, we finally went to the zoo to see the pandas.

The Stone Dragon

Early in the morning we left by bus for Badaling, an important mountain pass forty-five miles to the northwest of Beijing. The narrow two-lane road out of Beijing was clogged with bicycles, farm tractors, rattling horse-drawn wagons, pushcarts, pedestrians with heavy loads, and an occasional truck or bus.

We passed agricultural communes, market towns, and extensive rock quarries. We were soon in the mountains of the Yan Shan range, climbing and twisting over numerous horseshoe curves and tight switchbacks.

Then on the jagged, knife-edged ridge in the distance, "gamboling like a stone dragon over the northern hills, rising and falling in concert over the ridges and undulating far into the distance," was the Great Wall of China! It is so gigantic that it is earth's only man-made structure visible to the astronaut's eye from outer space. The brick and stone used in its construction could build a dike eight feet high circumscribing the earth.

Sections of the wall stretched along the very top of the mountain ridges like a massive gray ribbon laced along the spine of the green mountains. Finally we arrived at the post house in Chu Yung Pass. The sight exceeded all expectations. The wall averages twenty-one feet high and is eighteen feet wide at the top, broad enough to carry five cavalrymen or ten infantrymen abreast. It is broken at intervals with towers and guard houses. A continuous line of battlements along the north parapet face Mongolia.

The first section of the wall was begun as early as 403 BC, when a warlord barricaded his province against invaders. Other warring states built similar defenses. Two centuries before Christ, Qin Shi Huangdi (of Zi'an) unified China. He linked the separate sections of the wall and built new walls to form a 4,000-mile barrier across the north of China to keep out the nomadic barbarians of the Asian steppes. Today the Great Wall is 3,750 miles long and stretches over sixteen provinces.

Ms. Shih allowed us two hours to climb the wall. I went to the left and finally reached a high peak with a breathtaking view of Mongolia to the north. I stood there, trying to imagine the sound and fury of the storming hordes of Kublai Khan assaulting the wall, the blood and battles, and the centuries of conflict that the Great Wall had witnessed.

For more than eight centuries this massive defense was impenetrable. But China finally fell to an invader who simply bribed the sentries to open the gates. It is eternally true that the ultimate defense of a nation rests in the character of its people.

The Valley of the Tombs

When returning to Beijing, we turned into a serene valley basin to see the Royal Cemetery where thirteen emperors of the Ming Dynasty (1368-1644) are buried.

The Ming tombs are approached by a sacred way lined by gigantic camels, elephants, horses, and dragons—all carved from single blocks of white marble.

The individual tombs, scattered throughout the valley, are actually fortresslike underground stone palaces covered with a massive mountain of earth.

Beijing's Churches

When Chiang's Nationalist government capitulated and Mao's Communists took over in October 1949, chaos reigned in Beijing and throughout China. The central government had collapsed. There were no mail deliveries. Shops were closed for lack of goods and fear of looting. Banks closed, and money lost all value. Transportation ground to a halt. Communists entered the cities, towns, and villages to establish some semblance of order and structure.

At first the new regime reassured the people that there would be no interference with religion. In Beijing, people continued to attend church. Christian broadcasting continued. Students met freely. Christian meetings were held in schools and in classrooms.

However, this benevolent policy did not long endure. Sixty-five Christian churches were open in Beijing in 1949. By 1956 only four were left open. Congregations were consolidated, and vacated church properties were put to what the Communists called "productive use." Older pastors were persuaded to retire. Healthy young pastors were sent to work on state farms. Middle-aged pastors were assigned to factories.[1]

In 1966, at the beginning of the Cultural Revolution, Beijing's last four churches were closed, and the congregations were dispersed. In 1978, twelve years later, at the time of my first visit to Beijing, one Catholic and one Protestant church had been reopened. These showcase churches were intended to prove that freedom of religion did exist under the Mao regime.

I asked Ms. Shih to help me find these churches. She apologized, "I do not have permission to go with you." But Ms. Shih contracted a taxi for me and gave the driver the addresses.

The Catholics

At the Catholic church, the Immaculate Conception of the Blessed Mary, I met Father Michael Fu Tieshan. The cathedral would seat about five hundred. Father Michael said that attendance averaged "about fifty, mostly foreigners and tourists." The services were traditional in format and mass was said in Latin.

Father Michael and the Beijing church belong to the nationalized Catholic Patriotic Association, a breakoff church from the Vatican. I did not question him about persecutions, realizing this would be a sensitive subject to discuss with a stranger. I had read a recent report from the London-based Amnesty International that one bishop and thirty-six Jesuits were still in prison charged with counterrevolutionary activities.

The Chinese have a long history of confrontation with the Vatican over the issue of external control. Early in the eighteenth century, Catholicism was banned by the Emperor Kang Xi because of the Vatican's interference in internal church affairs. This resulted in 150 years of exclusion of Catholicism from China. By the turn of this century, Catholic missionaries were again in China.

Conflict with the Vatican erupted in 1932 when Japan invaded China and set up a puppet government in Manchukuo. The Vatican was the first to give diplomatic recognition to the puppet regime. The Pope ordered

Chinese Catholics not to interfere with the Japanese since the Japanese were fighting the Communist forces of Mao Zedong.

In the ensuing years, Chinese Catholics were under direct instructions from the Vatican to support the Nationalist cause and oppose the Communists. Many local priests and missionaries preferred neutrality. But the Catholic Church officially took an antirevolutionary position.

In 1949 there were an estimated three million Catholics in China. Clergy were estimated at 12,000, 5,500 being foreigners.[2] When the People's Republic of China was founded, the Vatican ordered faithful Chinese Catholics to be obstructionists, not to read newspapers, not to wear red scarves, not to participate in any Communist-organized or approved activity, and to oppose the new government in all ways possible.[3]

The pressure on Catholics was an appeal for patriotism. Patriotic Catholics were to renounce the foreign alliance with Rome and declare the Catholic Church of China independent and free from Vatican authority. Zhou Enlai stated in 1951. "To love one's fatherland is the duty of all, including Catholics."[4]

The Protestants had less difficulty in adapting to the concept of an independent Chinese church. Catholics continued to resist on the basis of fundamental doctrine. Rome was the head of the church. The Pope had authority given by Jesus Christ Himself, over the Church in China. To renounce this authority was to renounce the very essence of historic Catholic faith. As a result, there was much persecution of the Catholic resisters and dissidents who were loyal to Rome.

In the end, 166 foreign Catholic priests and missionaries either died in prison or were killed. Three hundred forty-six foreign Catholic missionaries had been imprisoned for periods ranging from two months to four years.[5] It is estimated that by 1954 between seven hundred and eight hundred Chinese priests lost their lives in the persecutions, as did unnumbered Catholic believers.[6]

The final break with the Vatican came in 1957, when a government-sponsored National Congress of Chinese Catholics met. The congress organized the Catholic Patriotic Association (a counterpart to the Three-Self Patriotic Protestant Church). The new Catholic Patriotic Church severed all ties with Rome.

In defiance of a direct prohibition from the Vatican, the Chinese Catholic Church proceeded to name its own bishops and ordain its own clergy. (In the Roman Catholic Church only the Pope is empowered to name a bishop and only ordination by the authority of Rome is valid.) For these actions, the Chinese clergy were excommunicated, and the Vatican has officially regarded the Catholic Patriotic Association as schismatic.

The Vatican's position with the Chinese Catholics continues to be "No compromise on Papal Authority." In November 1985, speaking to a group of bishops from Taiwan, Pope John Paul II continued to rebuke Chinese Catholic leaders who refused to accept his authority and said that a bond with the Roman pontiff is "essential for the faith of Catholics." He said that the Chinese Church had to be in communion with the universal church "with Peter and under Peter" to be authentic. (The Catholic Church considers the Pope a successor of Peter.)

A straightforward answer came immediately from China. Tang Ludao, secretary general of the China Catholic Patriotic Association, said, "For decades, the Vatican has pursued a policy of interference in China's internal affairs and disregarded the sovereignty of the Chinese Church. Under such circumstances, there can hardly be any relations between the Chinese Church and the Holy See. We are determined to change our longstanding colonial status and implement the guidelines of the Chinese Catholic Church: independence, self-reliance, and self-government."[7]

Beijing's Father Michael's parting word to me on that first visit in 1978 was, "The fires of faith have not died out in China."

Eight years later, I visited the Beijing Cathedral again. The attendance on Sunday is now two thousand and mass is scheduled four times daily with an average weekday attendance of two hundred.

On November 19, 1986 the Fourth Congress of the Catholic Patriotic Association met in Beijing. Bishop Zhong Huide reported that 1,900 Catholic Patriotic churches and other facilities (including 7 seminaries and 10 convents) have been reopened throughout China. In a direct challenge to the Vatican, the Catholic Patriotic Association of China, in the last three years, has elected and consecrated 22 bishops in 20 dioceses without the authority or approval of the Pope, including a Bishop Michael Fu Tieshan![8] The Patriotic Catholic churches now claim a membership of 700,000 communicants.

Chinese-consecrated Bishop Michael's prophecy has come true. The fires of an independent Chinese Catholic faith are burning brightly in China.

God Holds the Future

In 1978 I found the Beijing Protestant Church meeting in a large two-story gray stone building, which had housed the Bible Society before the revolution. Vice-President George Bush attended this church when he was U.S. liaison officer to China. The auditorium seated about two hundred.

I met the sixty-eight-year-old Pastor Yin Chi Chen, an Anglican, son of a Christian teacher and missionary. With him was Pastor Liu Chung Ho, a Presbyterian before the revolution. They told me that the church was closed at the beginning of the Cultural Revolution, and the pastors were sent to the farm to make a living.

After five years, the government allowed the church to reopen on Christmas Day 1971.

"Only one person came, a foreigner, an employee of the Pakistan Embassy," Pastor Yin recalled. "The Sunday attendance now averages four or five, mostly foreigners."

Pastor Yin said, "Since the Cultural Revolution, we have had no Chinese members."

I looked in vain for some evidence of despair or hopelessness.

"God's grace is great!" Pastor Yin said. "We must be faithful." His eyes glowed with hope and his voice was firm with commitment. "God holds our future in His hands!"

Over the next eight years in other visits to Beijing, I watched that future unfold. The tiny Protestant church (renamed the Beijing Christian Church) soon outgrew the Bible Society building. That facility now houses the national offices of the YMCA and the Three-Self Committee.

On Christmas Day 1982 the congregation moved to the former Asbury Methodist Church, a large building in the Chongwenmen district near the train station.

On my last visit to Beijing, I attended a Thursday morning Bible study in this church. "Our church has had seven hundred baptisms in the last three years," Pastor Kan Xueqing told me. A second pastor, Shi Zesheng, said, "We have opened a regional seminary in Beijing. We have seventeen students this first year, ten men and seven women, all from this church. Next year we will expand to receive students from the ten surrounding provinces." Pastor Kan, Pastor Shi, and other pastors from the pre-revolution period teach in the seminary. Courses include Greek, New Testament, Old Testament, theology, English, Chinese, and Chinese and biblical geography.

"How do you evaluate the current situation for Christianity?" I asked.

"In thirty years, this is the best time we have ever known. We have greater freedom today than we have ever had. And we are having greater results," Shi replied.

"Is there a direct confrontation with atheism?" I asked.

"There is conflict in thought, but not in the policy of the government. Neither the atheist nor the believer is to be discriminated against. That is the law. Today religion is not a point of conflict between individuals or with the government. Both the Christians and the atheists are needed in the total modernization effort of Chinese society. There is an acceptance of each other's right to freely believe or not to believe in God," Kan said.

"In this new atmosphere of freedom, are other religions growing?"

"Not like Christianity. Buddhism and Taoism do not appeal to young people. These religions have deep abstract concepts, are difficult to understand, and are mystical. On the other hand, Christianity is practical and down to earth in its application for living. Also, the Chinese have a great fascination for the Bible, just as they are fascinated with Western art, music, and culture. They know the Bible and Christianity are deeply woven into Western culture. Young people, especially, want to read the Bible in English not only to practice the language but also to understand the Bible. Chinese people find that the Bible provides a simple transmission of ideas that are easily understood and relate directly to life, like the Sermon on the Mount and the parables of Jesus," Shi said.

"What abut the Muslims?"

"Yes, there is a large Muslim minority in China, not only on the northwestern borders but scattered throughout China. They are easily identified by their customs and moral disciplines. They do not eat pork or drink alcohol. But whether they actually believe in all the tenets of Islam is a real question. For many whom I know, being Muslim is simply a form of traditional and disciplined living, and not a religious belief."

"Did you suffer for your faith in times past?" Both men told me the familiar story of harassment, abuse, separation from family, and assignment to work camps during the worst of the ultraleftist's reign of terror.

"Can this happen to Christians in China again?" I asked.

"There is no way that China will ever go back. They cannot close the churches down again. There is not the base of support in the government to do this. Those extreme leftist elements are no longer here," Kan said with certainty.

A Bible Woman's Sermon

While the Beijing Christian Church prospered, a second church opened in July 1980 in the city's west district, meeting in a former London Missionary Society church building, and calling itself the Gang Wa Shi Church. That church now has five pastors, three men and two women. It has an extensive program of Bible classes, prayer meetings, women's meetings, a sabbath meeting for the Adventists, plus sponsoring four extension house church meetings.

On my most recent visit to Beijing, I found a third Protestant church had just opened.

"Before 1949 the Chinese name of our church meant 'God is calling,'" deacon and church secretary Cai Lu Ping told me. "Now the congregation has taken the name 'Hadian,' the name of this area of Beijing." The church was reopened on the first Sunday in June 1985.

"The church was packed with three hundred people. It was a great day of rejoicing," lay evangelist and deacon Pan Tingovi told me.

At the Hadian Church on a Saturday afternoon, I heard an elderly

Bible woman, Ms. Xu Han Ming, conduct an old-time revival service. Several times during the sermon she broke into song (singing partially in English, for my benefit). She later told me that her father had been a pastor but had died of cancer. He told her to "carry on the work of the gospel." Now she is an evangelist and preaches to a house church congregation of two hundred people in the Western Hills section of Beijing. "As soon as we can find or construct a building, we will organize into a church," she said.

The latest estimate is that there are five thousand Christian believers in Beijing and thousands more in house churches in the outlying rural areas.

Farewell to Shih

On that first visit to Beijing, as we were leaving, our guide, Ms. Shih, wept unashamedly as she told us good-bye. She had begun to discuss Christianity freely with us, asking many questions about God, the Bible, and Jesus. I had offered her my English Bible, but she said it was forbidden for a guide to accept gifts.

As we walked to the steps to board our plane, we looked back at Ms. Shih with her black pigtails, white blouse, and blue slacks, standing at the rail of the observation platform, weeping and waving good-bye.

Two years later, I saw Ms. Shih again in the Beijing Duck Restaurant escorting another group of Americans. In "un-Chinese" exuberance, Ms. Shih hailed us across the room and rushed over to embrace us. A metamorphosis had occurred. Our plain, reserved Mongolian goatherder was no more. In her high heels, black silk dress, and chic hairdo, she was an enchanting beauty. Her transformation was even more obvious as she talked. Ms. Shih left her group to eat with us, bubbling in animated conversation.

"You know about 'Death by Duck'?" Ms. Shih asked with a twinkle in her eye as I took another serving. Tourists come to Beijing, climb the Great Wall in the afternoon, gorge on roast duck and bean sauce in the evening, and die of a heart attack in the hotel that night. She cautioned me, "Yes, it is true."

With Ms. Shih was a friend, Wang Lu-ching, an English student and history major from the Beijing Iron and Steel Institute. When Ms. Shih introduced me as a pastor, our conversation turned to religion.

"What do you mean God is power . . . God is light . . . God is love?" Ms. Wang asked, taking a paperback Gospel of John from her bag. "A Swedish woman gave it to me," Ms. Wang explained.

"She also taught me a Christian song." When I pressed her, Ms. Wang sang in a soft soprano voice,

> I am sailing over the sea.
> Over life's troubled seas.
> Sailing to come home to you.
> To be free, to be free.
> Oh, Lord, I want to come to you and be free.

I took a New Testament from my camera bag and asked Ms. Shih, "Would you like to have it?"

"Oh, yes, yes!"

"Before, you told me it was forbidden," I said.

She smiled, "Everything is different now."

Ms. Shih, the little Mongolian goatherder, was different. The new China was different. Deng's modernization programs were beginning to lock into place. Headlines and stories in my miscellaneous clippings file document the changing China.

An eighteen-hole golf course costing eleven million dollars has been built in the sacrosanct Ming Valley near the tomb of Emperor Ding Ling. (China's last golf course was plowed under in 1949, the game denounced as a perverted capitalistic "sport of millionaires.") A horse-racing track, aquarium, and Disney-style amusement park are planned for Beijing. Coca Cola, discos, sidewalk fast-food stalls, souvenir shops selling religious articles, cloisonne crosses, and ceramic Madonnas can easily be found.

Helicopter rides over the Great Wall cost ten dollars American money. An entrepreneur offers a ride on a Bactrian (two-humped) camel for one yuan, a picture for two yuan. Souvenir stands sell T-shirts proclaiming,

"I climbed the Great Wall of China." Five busloads of Christians leave
Beijing at four o'clock AM for a public Easter sunrise service on the
Great Wall.

The Forbidden City swarms with free-lance photographers and artists. Boys peddle "antique" coins, "very cheap." Lemonade stands have
gaudy, striped beach umbrellas, and Popsicle wagons abound. Two soldiers ask for a Bible on the Imperial Palace steps.

A four-lane express highway leads to the Great Wall. In Beijing six-
lane thoroughfares have giant "flyovers" (overpasses) and "spaghetti"
junctions. Traffic jams are commonplace, and sixty-seven people were
killed in traffic accidents in one month in Beijing.

The Beijing subway is under construction following a route under-
neath the ancient city walls. Among the high-rise apartments, office
buildings, and hotels is Beijing's new, flamboyant Great Wall Hotel with
a six-story atrium lobby, 1,007 luxury rooms, and computerized check-
in. Two more churches are scheduled to reopen in Beijing soon.

Detroit delivered a fleet of twenty Cadillac limousines to Beijing to
"impress visiting businessmen." When private enterprise photocopy
service sold stock in the venture, $17.50 per share (a half-month's
wage), thousands lined up to buy. Merrill-Lynch helped China's National Bank set up a stock exchange in Shanghai. McGraw-Hill and Chinese partners launched a Chinese version of *Business Week*. National
congresses on religion were conducted in Beijing by both Catholics and
Protestants.

A British rock group, WHAM, gave a concert in China. Arthur Mill-
er's *Death of a Salesman* was performed in a Beijing theater. A bus
driver played Willie Nelson country music tapes while we waited at the
Great Wall. *The Pilgrim's Progress* was published in English and sold
out in two days.

Hotels are planned for the Forbidden City to use some of the nine
thousand ancient rooms of the Imperial Palace. "The Empress of China
slept here" is the gimmick. Three clerks in Beijing's Friendship Store
say they are "Christians too."

Beijing encourages doctors and dentists to "go private" to "upgrade
the quality of medical care in China." Sixty-one thousand free markets,

looking like bazaars elsewhere, are operating throughout China. Registered private enterprises stand at 11.7 million (compared to 7.2 million private businesses when the Communists took power in 1949). Beijing has announced that the "Iron Rice Bowl" is broken—no more guaranteed pay and lifetime employment because jobs and wages will be based on productivity. Three million urban workers in state enterprises signed production contracts in lieu of fixed wages. Deng appeared on Chinese television and encouraged young men to leave the farm, to go to the city, and to become entrepreneurs and start businesses. Chinese Protestant believers in four thousand open churches exceeded 4 million, more than five times the seven hundred thousand at the end of the missionary era in 1949.

"Yes, Shih, things are different," I said and gave her the Bible.

Notes

1. A. J. Dain, *Mission Fields Today* (London: Intervarsity Fellowship, 1956), pp. 21-22.

2. *Current Affairs Journal,* No. 3, 1950. Reproduced by Beijing NCNA, November 23, 1950.

3. C. P. Fitzgerald, *The Birth of Communist China* (Harmondsworth, Middlesex: Penguin Books, Ltd.; Baltimore, MD: Penguin Books, 1964), p. 135.

4. George N. Patterson, *Christianity in Communist China* (Waco: Word, Inc., 1969) p. 102.

5. Thomas J. Bauer, M. M., *The Systematic Destruction of the Catholic Church in China* (New York: World Horizon Reports, 1954).

6. Union Research Service, Hong Kong, October 11, 1955, p. 1.

7. Tang Ludao in Associated Press dispatch, November 10, 1985.

8. Beijing's Xinhua News Agency, as reported in the *Miami Herald,* International Edition, November 20, 1986.

7

Center of Learning
Shanghai

Flying into Shanghai is a beautiful experience. The city lies in the estuary of the world's third longest river, the mighty Yangtze. From the air the vast rich delta looks like a giant leaf, splotched in green and brown and veined by twisting rivers and canals.

Dropping lower, one sees a crazy-quilt pattern of the dikes and fields, canals and compounds, and low-lying hills. There are red-tiled roofs and tree-lined roads and water storage ponds covered with iridescent algae. The canals are choked with barges and boats.

As the delta unrolls like a brilliant tapestry, one sees Shanghai on the horizon, a sprawling expanse of buildings and streets that straddles the muddy river. On the river, scattered like leaves on a millpond, are ships of every flag from the four corners of the earth. The traffic of the seas stretches as far as the eye can see out to the place where the weary Yangtze casts its burden of amber silt into the blue of the East China Sea.

The Sinner's Paradise

Shanghai! The city's name is both a noun and a verb. The very word conjures up images of kidnapped sailors and mysterious intrigue, coolie-drawn rickshas and Englishmen in white pith helmets, women in slit-skirted silk and smoke-filled opium dens, beggars and thieves, Oriental gangsters, and elegant opulence.

Precommunist Shanghai reigned as the Empress of the Orient, the financial and trading giant of the East, fast, loose, and freewheeling. Wicked and festering in corruption beyond imagination, the city had a

126

singular reputation as a "paradise for sinners," where every known vice could be found in the murky underworld.

A Fishing Village

Shanghai was little more than an insignificant fishing village until seven hundred years ago. At that time, the Ming Dynasty built a fortress on the banks of the river to block the interior from marauding Japanese pirates.

Shanghai remained a relatively indistinct trading port until 1842, when the British fleet sailed up the river and shelled the city. Shanghai surrendered and the water gateway to the lucrative internal markets of China was forced to open to Western trade.

Other European countries followed Britain. Shanghai was carved up by the colonial powers, each claiming exclusive rights over a section of the city. This established the alien-ruled International Concessions. Residents in the foreign enclaves were exempt from Chinese law and taxes. Chinese were forbidden to enter the concessions without a permit. Even the Chinese who worked for colonial masters paid a toll to enter.

The Colonial Era

In the century that followed, trade and commerce flourished. Industry expanded. The population exploded, spawning vast slums rampant with indescribable poverty and human deprivation.

One account of the extremity of the human misery tells how the gutters of Shanghai during the winter were "littered with the corpses of the poor who had died the previous night from exposure and starvation, while nearby the wealthy could be seen using sable rugs to cover the motors of their parked limousines."[1]

The presence of the hated foreigners in the concessions, the desperate plight of the masses of urban poor, the arrogant display of compassionless wealth, and an insensitive government fueled the fires of discontent and revolution. The organized expression of Communism in China was born in Shanghai when the first party congress was held on July 23,

1921, in an ordinary resident's home. The modest gray brick row house is a tourist attraction today.

The Chaotic Decade

During the decade before 1949, Shanghai was devastated by a series of catastrophes. In 1937 the Japanese captured Shanghai and for eight long years held the city in a brutal military occupation. Following the defeat of the Japanese, Shanghai was wracked by workers' strikes and violent street demonstrations which were broken up by Nationalist troops, desperately attempting to stabilize the government.

Economic distress was horrendous. Inflation reached tragic dimensions. A lifetime of savings could be wiped out overnight and would not buy even a pound of rice. The Chinese yuan became so worthless that one dollar bought three million yuan, a wheelbarrow full of paper money. Official corruption and greed abounded.

That was the Shanghai of 1949, a city of five million people, devastated by civil war, economic collapse, moral decay, and political instability. The Empress of the Orient had become a shabby lady without a throne when Mao's government took control.

The Big Apple

Thirty-five years under the People's Republic of China have seen a new Shanghai emerge. Shanghai is now a booming industrial and commercial city with eight thousand factories. One half of all Chinese internal and external commerce passes through the city by water, rail, air, and oceangoing vessels.

The city has not changed in one respect. Shanghai is still the most Westernized city in China, the "New York of Asia," throbbing, dynamic, sophisticated. Walking the streets, one senses an urbane vitality, a spirit of enterprise, competition, vigor, and youth (the average age is twenty-four years). One third of the people on the streets of the central city do not live in Shanghai but come in to do business or to work. At the heart of the city is the Bund, the former Wall Street of China, a tree-lined promenade along the waterfront, flanked by Victorian gray stone buildings.

Shanghai is China's cultural and entertainment center and the fashion trend setter for the rest of the country. Nanjing Road is Shanghai's "Fifth Avenue," with stylish shops, restaurants, theaters, and China's largest department store. Shanghai women are reputed to be the best dressed in China.

Recently the French designer Pierre Cardin was invited to China by the government to act as a consultant on Chinese fashions. Deng appeared on Chinese television urging women to look more feminine and dress more femininely. Today the traditional cheongsam (the tight dress with the high mandarin collar and slit skirt) is in style again. It had been banned thirty years ago as decadently "bourgeois" and had been replaced by baggy blue proletarian pantaloons.

On a harbor cruise to the junction of the Yangtze, one sees the fascinating mixture of old and new. Working junks, their lugsails like weathered tents opened to the wind, out past oceangoing freighters, leviathans of the deep, moving slowly out to sea. An oscillating, webbed radar guides the freighter along, while the giant eyes of the river's good spirit painted on the prow "guide" the Chinese junk.

The Yu Yuan Gardens, built just after Columbus discovered America, are said to be the most beautiful in the Orient. An imperial mandarin named Yu laid out a garden to duplicate all China's scenery—mountains, gorges, caves, rivers, and lakes—in miniature within his own backyard. The garden is a marvel and model of park planning even today.

Nearby is the "old town," modern Shanghai's own Chinatown. The tangle of narrow lanes, tiny shops, and ancient gardens is a picture of the city as it was before the colonial era.

Shanghai is China's largest city, with 12 million people. The central city area has a population of 6.4 million, the most densely populated area in the world. The suffocating population density is 100 thousand people per square mile, four times that of Tokyo and ten times that of New York.

China's Time Bomb

Futurologists say that China cannot survive as a nation unless the population growth is brought under control. In the past thirty years, the population has almost doubled to a billion. There is simply not enough tillable land and food to care for any more people. Mao's regime failed completely to come to grips with China's exploding population problem.

In 1979 a tough one-child-per-family program was initiated and is enforced by a system of rewards and penalties. Free education, free medical services, discounts on food and clothing, promotions at work, and allocation of better apartments are the rewards for single-child couples.

Additional children bring severe penalties, fines, loss of all benefits, loss of job and housing. There is an agressive promotion of contraceptives and abortion as a means of birth control. Street committees in every neighborhood pressure couples to have only one child. Abortions may now outnumber live births in China.

Sociologists are anxious about the future implications of the one-child policy. Their fear is that the nation is producing a new generation of pampered, selfish, overprotected, lonely children. As self-centered, spoiled, only-child adults they will be poor partners in marriage as well as poor citizens of a collective society based on putting the interests of the group ahead of those of the individual.

Another concern is economic. Life expectancy is up from thirty-two years in 1949 to sixty-four years today. Many more elderly people are surviving. In the next generation, one working couple will eventually find themselves saddled with four elderly nonworking parents and perhaps grandparents. The one working couple will not be able to produce a sufficient salary to personally carry this economic burden. Neither can the work force generate enough taxes for the government to support so many elderly people.

A third problem is already apparent: Males outnumber females. The Chinese have always preferred male children, especially in rural families. Boys guarantee the continuity of the family line. In the past, boys have remained with the family, cared for the elderly parents, and were income-producing. Girls were considered a liability.

In the past in rural areas, killing unwanted baby girls was a common practice. A bucket of water was kept by the mother's bed as she was giving birth. If the newborn were a girl, the infant was immediately drowned. Today, with the enforcement of the one-child policy, evidence shows that this practice is being revived, in spite of severe penalties and strong opposition by the government.

Center of Learning

Early in the colonial period, Shanghai became a center for Western-styled education.

Timothy Richards, pioneer British Baptist missionary who went to China in 1870, founded the first public school for Chinese in Shanghai. He also established the University of Shensi. In 1905 Northern and Southern Baptists and Chinese Baptists established Shanghai University.

It is ironic that the single largest monument to Mao Zedong in Shanghai today is a thirty-foot tall statue standing at the entrance to Tongji University. Mao had a basic disdain for education and expertise. He always felt that the intellectuals were the enemy of the revolution.

Historically the educated have always been a distinct elite in China, clearly apart from common people. Confucius taught that scholarship was the highest form of virtue. Mencius, who lived three centuries before Christ, said, "He who uses his mind rules; he who uses his hands is ruled." During most of China's history the scholars formed the government bureaucracy that ran the country for the emperor. Mao's peasant revolution sought to erase that gap by eradicating the intellectuals and establishing a single peasant/worker-class society.

One of Mao's first acts after 1949 was to close all liberal arts universities. Mao felt that bourgeois social science was contradictory to the Marxist revolution. When everyone became workers there would be no more exploitation between the classes and no more economic inequities. Therefore, liberal arts universities were closed; professors who taught political science, economics, history, or sociology were put through a period of reeducation. They were sent to the farms or factories to become workers. University students went through the same reeducation process. Many were sent to the furthest outposts in Tibet or Inner Mongolia or to the most barren, poverty-stricken environments. The schools later reopened as technical and industrial institutes. For example, Shanghai University became the Shanghai Institute of Mechanical Engineering (SIME).

The Final Blow

"The final blow to education came with the Cultural Revolution which left schools a total disaster area," said a Chinese physicist, Dr. Huang Weifeng.[2]

The Cultural Revolution began in 1966 when Mao Zedong turned the Red Guards loose on the people. Militant youth of the Communist party set out to destroy everything "old," including the old superstructures of society. Since the revolution was based on manual labor, any other activity was considered nonproductive; those engaged in such activity were either reeducated or eliminated.

All segments of society were attacked—public officials, military people, doctors, lawyers, professors, and clergymen. Public accusation meetings were held. The victims were ridiculed, shamed, often beaten and abused, and then sent to the farms or factories to become material producers for society.

A misspoken word or a careless act could bring the charge of being a decadent "bourgeois" or a "feudal" adherent. For example, a group of students asked a university professor to dismiss class so they could join in a street demonstration. He refused, saying, "You came to school to learn, not to demonstrate." That one remark was the basis for his being exiled and sentenced to a work farm for reeducation as an anti-revolutionary.

The possession of a radio or camera at home or possessing a book or printed matter in a foreign language was proof enough for some to accuse a person of being a spy or foreign agent. Parents dared not reprimand their children lest they be reported, denounced, and punished for being antirevolutionary. People were dragged into the streets for a "struggle session": to be humiliated, shouted at, insulted, and beaten by the howling tormentors. The aim was to get a "confession" or at least to "improve" their attitude.

Young people were gathered by the thousands, loaded onto trains, and shipped to the country to work as peasants in the fields to "recapture the revolutionary spirit." The present government estimates that 10 percent of the population was displaced and moved during the terrible decade of the Cultural Revolution. Some historians say that this was the largest forced migration of people in human history.

Mao's Cultural Revolution closed all the universities and schools. The whole educational system of China was essentially dismantled for ten years. A typical example of the carnage from that era can be seen in statistics from the University of Beijing, one of China's most prestigious institutions. Of the 177 professors on the faculty at that time, 145 were eliminated, punished, jailed, or deported to labor camps where many died or committed suicide in despair.[3] The result was the crippling of a nation badly in need of an educated leadership and scientific and management skills. Virtually all study and research halted.

One hundred million people, by government count, ended up illiterate because of that ten-year disruption in the educational system and the interruption of their lives at the crucial time when they should have been in school. This was "China's Holocaust," as one Chinese said; the effects were worse than any war the country had ever experienced. "We lost a whole generation," a Chinese professor said to me.

The Lost Generation

Chang Tiekong was one of that lost generation. Chang was in high school at the beginning of the Cultural Revolution. His mother was a middle-school teacher, and Chang was scheduled to attend the university. But the schools were closed, and Chang was sent to the west to a farm in Anhui Province. He lived in a dormitory on corn porridge and rice with meat only once a month.

"The work was terribly hard, seven days a week, daylight to dark, for no salary. I was to 'experience' the life of the peasant," he told me. "Every morning before going to the fields, I was forced to stand in front of a picture of Mao and for thirty minutes read aloud to him from his 'sayings.' It was like praying to him and promising that I would practice his teachings that day. Again at night, I had to do the same thing. It was terrible, as though Mao were God and I was confessing to him all I had done wrong that day and asking for his forgiveness."

After four long years at the labor camp, Chang was transferred back to Shanghai and assigned to a watch factory to "experience" the life of a city worker.

The Cultural Revolution denied Chang an opportunity for an education. Nevertheless, he was determined to improve himself and went to night school to learn English. In 1984 Chang applied for a job as a clerk working with tourists.

"I do not get any more pay than I did in the factory, but it is better work. I am able to meet people from all over the world and learn about things outside China. The greatest thing is that on this job I became a Christian believer." Chang went on to tell me how an American tourist had given him a Bible and Christian literature. He and two of his fellow clerks, a young woman named Pi and a young man named Zhong, had also become believers by reading the material.

Chang is now married. His pay is one hundred yuan a month (about sixty dollars). Six yuan goes for rent and utilities and thirty yuan for food. That leaves sixty-four yuan for all other items: clothing, household furnishing, personal items, and the needs of their two-year-old son.

"Today, we have economic problems in China," Chang admitted. "But these are happy days. We have freedom now, and it is so wonderful."

Deng's Reforms

One of Deng's priorities was to reform and modernize education. A new law, taking effect July 1, 1986, requires nine years of compulsory education for all of China's young people: six years at the primary level and three years of junior high. English is a required course and, if this policy continues, will become China's second language in another generation.

One of Deng's first actions was to change the method whereby students were selected for admission to the universities. Under Mao, students were required first to labor as a peasant or factory worker and to be ideologically "correct" to be eligible for university training. Party loyalty and not academic ability was the sole qualification. Deng reinstituted the open admission policy based on academic testing. The first year 5.5 million young people took university entrance exams, which was 25 applicants for each opening. Presently there are 520 universities and colleges that can confer bachelor's degrees, 425 schools and research institutes that can confer master's degrees, and 196 institutions that can confer doctor's degrees.[4]

While China is making great strides in education, the nation has a long way to go by comparison to Western standards. In 1980 in the U.S., for example, 3,540 per 10,000 of the population received a higher education of some kind, while in China the figure was only 9 per 10,000.

There is clearly a trend back to traditional education values in China. The emphasis is shifting from the worker back to the intellectual and student. In a recent poll of one thousand Chinese students regarding their choice of a vocation, university teaching was first, then medicine, natural science, and electrical engineering.

There is also renewed interest in the liberal arts. The Shanghai Institute of Mechanical Engineering (the former Shanghai University) has signed a contract with a consultant from Baylor University to study the curriculum and propose additional courses that would broaden the cultural base of the institute's program. An interesting sidelight on the broadening taking place in Chinese higher education is that in a Nanjing university the autobiography of Lee A. Iacocca is a part of the required reading in a course on American culture.[5]

"Private universities are springing up in the big cities of China," Dr. C. K. Chang of Anhui Normal University told me. There is a volunteer board of directors "like before liberation." Usually the building is donated by a wealthy individual. The faculty are part-time teachers from the government universities or retired professors who are interested in developing a higher quality of education. They also receive a modest salary, which helps, "because our regular salary is rather low." Brighter and more highly motivated students who really want to study attend and pay tuition. The graduates are free to choose their jobs rather than being assigned a job by the state because the state has not paid for their education. "They are in great demand because they are better motivated and trained," Chang told me.[6]

The Churches of Shanghai

Shanghai became a center for the Christian ministry when the city was opened to Western trade 140 years ago. Missionaries followed the traders up the Yangtze River.

Five years after the British fleet took Shanghai, the first Baptist missionaries, J. Lewis and Eliza Sexton Shuck and Matthew T. and Eliza Moving Yates, began work in Shanghai. In their first year on the field, on November 6, 1847 they organized the Old Northgate Baptist Church with two Chinese converts as members. During the century that followed, Shanghai became the base for the deployment of missionaries of all denominations. Christianity spread to the principal cities throughout the Yangtze basin and up and down the east China coast.

In 1905 Shanghai University, a joint project of Northern and Southern Baptist missionaries, was established and soon began graduating Christian leaders from all parts of China.

Four hundred miles to the north of Shanghai, near the coastal city of Yantai (Chefoo), is Penglai, where the legendary Baptist missionary Lottie Moon worked. In that province of Shandong, the famous Shantung Revivals of the 1930s took place. All along the east coast of China—to the north, the south, and up the rivers into the interior—fields were "ripe unto harvest" for the gospel. Many churches were built, and Christianity flourished in East China with Shanghai as the hub.

The Winter of Tribulation

On August 8, 1966, the Chinese Communist Party Central Committee adopted the "Decision Concerning the Great Proletarian Cultural Revolution." A few days later a poster appeared at the entrance of a former YMCA building presaging what lay ahead for the churches. It read:

There is no God, there is no Spirit; there is no Mary; there is no Joseph. How can adults believe in these things. . . . Priests live in luxury and . . . like Islam and Catholicism, Protestantism is a reactionary feudal ideology, the opium of the people, with foreign origins and contacts. . . . We are atheists; we believe only in Mao Zedong. We call on all people to burn Bibles, destroy images and disperse religious associations.[7]

Two weeks after the Central Committee passed the resolution that launched the Cultural Revolution, the *South China Morning Post* of Hong Kong documented what happened. The August 24, 1966, headline read "Christianity in Shanghai Comes to an End." The article said that the final chapter of the history of the Christian religion in Shanghai had been written eight days earlier. On that day "all churches were stripped of crosses, statues, icons and decorations by revolutionary students wearing Red Guard armbands and determined to eradicate all traces of imperialist, colonial and feudal regimes." Bibles, hymnals, books used in religious services, religious tracts, and items found in the archives of the churches were burned in bonfires in front of the churches. Among the Shanghai churches burned or vandalized were the Roman Catholic Cathedral, the Anglican Cathedral, and the Mu'en (formerly Moore Memorial Methodist) Church.[8]

There were two hundred Protestant churches in Shanghai in 1949. Mao reduced those to twenty-three in 1958 during the "Great Leap Forward." In 1966 Red Guards closed the last of those churches and Shanghai Christians suffered greatly.

The torrent of Red Guard violence swept like an all consuming fire into every part of China. The sufferings of one pastor in Central China were described by his wife: "They burned all the books in my husband's library, our family photo album, our paintings, our furniture, in a big bonfire in front of our house. We both were made to kneel in the streets, while they harangued and shouted at us. They cut my hair off and hung a placard around my husband's neck that read 'I am a Christian reactionary!' They beat his head and shoulders with a stick demanding he confess his crimes, but he just bowed his head and prayed to God all the time."

She was put to work in a factory cleaning toilets, and her husband was sent far away to work in Hunan Province. When he arrived, all his belongings except the clothes on his back were confiscated. He lived in the most primitive conditions, sleeping on the mud floor of an empty warehouse. He was never allowed to take a bath more than once a month. He worked in the fields every day.[9]

For thirteen years the churches of Shanghai were closed. Pastors languished in prison or did hard labor on farms and in factories. The congregations were dispersed, and Christianity was a secret and hidden faith. Pastor Sun Yanli of the Mu'en Church worked in a Shanghai factory. When Deng's new government came into power, Pastor Sun and a group of other Christians petitioned the government for the return of the church property to the congregation.

The Return of Spring

Wang Weifan, a Shanghai pastor, wrote a hymn that is a favorite among Chinese Christians today.

> Winter is passed, the rain is o'er
> Earth is a-bloom, songs fill the air.
> Linger no more, why must you wait
> Rise up my love, come follow me.
> CHORUS:
> Jesus my Lord, my love, my all
> Body and soul, forever yours
> In dale so dark, I long for thee
> Spring has returned, abide with me.[10]

Spring came at last for the Christians of Shanghai. On September 2, 1979, Mu'en Church was reopened for public worship. More than two thousand people jammed the building designed to seat twelve hundred "they were in the aisles, doorways, windows, and out into the courtyard, singing, weeping, and rejoicing," I was told. Today the church has three weekend services, with more than six thousand people in attendance.

Shortly thereafter the former International Community Church in the old French Concession area reopened. The pastor, Shen Yifan, told me that since opening the church has baptized more than seven hundred new members, including many young people. The church now has five pastors, a fifty-member choir, and an active weekday ministry of Bible classes, reading classes in English and Chinese, and women's meetings. On Sunday morning there are two services, both packed with one thousand in the sanctuary and eight hundred in overflow rooms watching by closed-circuit television.

A few months later the Grace Church (formerly a Baptist church) was reopened. The building had been used as a factory for fourteen years. Pastor Chou Lien Fu told me that the church has six pastors and eleven other church workers. Like all other churches, it is entirely supported by offerings from the members. The building required thirty-five thousand dollars worth of repair before it could be reoccupied, "We borrowed the money and have paid back every bit of it. Our people are very sacrificial in their giving," Pastor Chou said.

The church has three services each weekend, including a Saturday morning service with a total attendance of fifty-five hundred. The church has baptized twelve hundred converts since reopening and has a large number in the "inquirers" class. Pastor Chou said, "So many, especially young people, have no Christian background. It is necessary to have a thorough doctrinal training program for new converts before they are baptized. But they are all eager to learn."

I witnessed the eagerness of Chinese Christians in a Bible study at Grace Church on a Tuesday evening. A remarkable number of young people were part of the large congregation. Everyone had a Bible of some shape, form, or condition. Pastor Chang Chincou led with a big flipchart, a pointer, and a microphone.

The service opened with the hymn "Jesus Is All the World to Me," and then Pastor Chang taught the congregation a new song, "line by line." I recognized the song as "Lord, I'm Coming Home." After a prayer, the Bible study began in earnest as Pastor Chang vigorously exhorted and pointed to references on the chart. The audience, to the last person, followed in their Bibles, reading intently and rapidly writing in their notebooks.

After an hour the study was over, and the group stood to sing, "When Jesus comes, . . . will He find us watching?" Pastor Chang's comment to me after the service seemed almost unnecessary: "The Chinese people love the Bible."

Gospel Explosion

Today twenty-two churches are open in Shanghai in addition to many meeting places and house churches where Christians also gather. "We have thirty-five thousand active Christians in Shanghai attending services on Sunday," Pastor Chou told me. That is coming from zero seven years ago. Nor does that include an estimated fifteen thousand inactive Christians who for one reason or another do not or cannot attend a public service. That makes the Christian population of Shanghai an estimated fifty thousand believers only seven years after the Mu'en Church opened in September 1979.

As astounding and remarkable as these statistics may seem, there are large rural areas in China where Christianity is exploding at an even more phenomenal rate. In Zhejiang Province, just south of Shanghai, many fishing villages on the coast are reported to be solidly Christian. Today there are 750,000 Protestant Christians in this province, which is more than all the Christians in the whole of China in 1949.

Life-Style Evangelism

I asked Pastor Chou at Grace Church, "How can this happen in an officially 'atheistic' country?"

"There are not many real, hard-core, militant atheists among the common people," Chou replied. "The Chinese people, deep down in their hearts, know there is a God. They want to live moral lives and be good citizens. They know there is something else beyond this life. They know God is the only answer to the problem of their lives. Not even all the Communists are atheists. When they hear the gospel, it has great power to lead them to believe."

I asked Han Wenzao, of the China Christian Council, about this geometric explosion of Christianity. It had come without radio, television, advertising, promotion, street services, door-to-door visitation, evangelistic crusades, and primarily without large public services. "In our American churches we consider these implementations absolutely necessary for effective evangelism," I said.

"It has been by the 'power of God,'" Han answered. Then, pausing, he added, "And by 'life-style evangelism.' We Chinese believe life-style evangelism is the most effective and authentic kind of evangelism. By living their faith, Chinese Christians witness that theirs is a 'different' way of life. It is a sermon in a life, not just a sermon in a pulpit."

Life-style evangelism! Back at the Shanghai Hotel, I saw the evidence of "life-style evangelism." A young clerk in the silk shop noticed the tiny gold cross pinned on my wife's blouse.

"Are you a Christian?" she asked. As Lealice replied, "Yes," the girl continued, "I know a Christian family. They live in the same building where I live. They are so different. The husband does not drink or beat his wife. She does not yell at him and fight. They are so kind to everyone. Their marriage is so happy."

She went on to say, "I think it is because they are Christians." She was newly married. "I wish I could have a marriage like that. Does your Bible tell how to become a Christian and live like that?"

After she had been given two Bibles, one for herself and one for her husband, she said, "I am so happy. Now I can learn how to become a Christian and live a good life like theirs."

Notes

1. Fredric Kaplan/Julian Sobin/Arne de Keijzer, *The China Guide Book*, 1985 edition (Houghton Mifflin Co.), Boston, p. 500.

2. Dr. Wei-Feng Huang, "U of L Professor Gets Regal Treatment," *Louisville Times*, October 11, 1978, p. C-18.

3. Ibid.

4. Britt Towery, "China Education New," *China Journal*, June 1986, p. 4.

5. As reported in *International Herald Tribune*, September 20, 1986.

6. C. K. Chang, interview.

7. Britt Towery, Jr., *The Churches of China* (Hong Kong: Amazing Grace books, 1986), p. 21.

8. *South China Morning Post*, Hong Kong, August 26, 1966.

9. Ralph Lohne, "China Report," *In Ministry*, September 1980, p. 5.

10. Wang Weifan, "I'll Follow Thee," Towery, p. 83.

9

Bridge Over Troubled Waters

Nanjing (Nanking)

Nanjing is a city of bridges!

From antiquity, China's rivers have been her highways. The mighty Yangtze is China's greatest river, third longest in the world, surpassed only by the Nile and the Amazon. The headwaters of the Yangtze rise in Tibet and are fed by the glaciers and perpetual snows of the eighteen-thousand foot Tangula Mountains. The river cuts from west to east across nine provinces in a wild rush to the East China Sea, dividing China into the North and the South. Eighty percent of all inland water traffic plies her waters. Oceangoing vessels penetrate six hundred miles upstream to the docks at Hanyang.

A vast system of canals crisscrosses the Yangtze basin, feeding rich, nourishing waters into the fertile Eastern Plains. The wide alluvial basin, averaging six hundred miles in width, extends for two thousand miles across China. The basin produces 70 percent of the nation's rice, one-third of the cotton, and half of the tea. The bulk of China's one billion people live in the Yangtze basin.

In season, the mighty Yangtze is China's lifegiving blessing. In floodtime, the river is China's devastating curse and sorrow. From time immemorial the angry floodwaters of the Yangtze have periodically broken its banks, sweeping away crops, houses, and millions of lives. The bridge in Nanjing that crosses the violent and troubled waters of the mighty Yangtze is the consummate pride of all China, a world-renowned engineering triumph.

Big Brother's Failure

"Formerly it took two hours by ferry to transfer a train across the river. Now a train crosses in two minutes," our guide, Mr. Lieu, told us in the reception room atop one of the massive piers. Today the two-tiered, four-mile-long bridge carries 180 trains and 10,000 vehicles a day across the Yangtze, linking Shanghai and south China with Beijing and north China. While the bridge makes a substantial contribution to the economy of China, its symbolism may be even more significant.

"The Russians spent ten years trying to build the bridge for us. They gave up in 1960 and went home, taking their blueprints and engineering studies with them," Mr. Lieu said disparagingly. The broad, flood-prone seventy-foot-deep, silt-laden river flows over a slick bedrock floor, creating a problem that defied the ingenuity of Soviet engineering.

The Chinese tackled the problem on their own. In eight years they accomplished the impossible and built this engineering marvel. Seven thousand laborers worked on the project. The bridge cost $280 million (in 1960 U.S. dollars). One hundred thousand tons of steel and one million tons of concrete were used in the construction.

"We did what the Russians couldn't do," Mr. Lieu said with pride. For the Chinese, the Nanjing Bridge conquered more than the Yangtze River. It is a symbolic victory over the Russians!

The Dragon and the Bear

Contemporary China has looked to the Soviets as its ideological mentor. The political philosophy of Karl Marx that powered the Soviet revolution was also the driving force in Mao's revolution. Dr. Sun Yatsen, father of the Chinese Republic, found an ally in the Soviet Communists. Chiang Kaishek, in earlier days, assimilated the Communists into his army, only to expel them later. Mao Zedong found his inspiration in the Bolshevik revolution and gained support from the Soviet Union in the civil war against Chiang's Nationalists.

Within forty-eight hours after the birth of the People's Republic of China in 1949, Stalin granted diplomatic recognition to Mao's government. Mao was immediately invited to Moscow where a thirty-year treaty of friendship was signed.

The breakup of the union came in 1960 when China opened a propaganda attack on Soviet Communism. An angry Khrushchev withdrew all Soviet technical advisers from China, including those working on the Yangtze River Bridge project in Nanjing. Other incompleted projects all over China were abandoned.

The Soviet connection was never really popular with the Chinese people. "We soon got enough of them," Dr. C. K. Chang told me. "In the early days after liberation, the regime was very dogmatic. 'We must copy everything from the Soviets,' they said. All other foreign languages, including English, were banned from the schools. Only Russian was taught. Russian is a difficult language, and nobody wanted to learn it. Many of the Russian textbooks that we were required to use had been translated from the German or English to Russian. Many of our professionals already knew German and English. It made us dislike all things Russian even more."[1]

When I was visiting the Guangzhou truck plant, the manager, Mr. Chung, pointed to a piece of equipment. "China bought a machine from East Germany to be delivered by train through the Soviet Union. But our friends, the Russians, kept the new machinery and shipped us this old, broken-down piece of used equipment. Typically Russian, 'our friends in word, but not in deed,'" he said.

The Chinese will never forget that they also paid heavily for Soviet friendship by granting the Soviet Union temporary control of Manchuria's ports and railways and forfeited the Chinese claim to Outer Mongolia.

Today trouble continues to smolder all along the Chinese-Soviet border where both countries keep a sizable contingent of soldiers. Bloody clashes erupt periodically.

The Southern Capital

Nanjing is a charming city in the foothills of the Zijin (purple) Mountains. Giant sycamores, like umbrellas, canopy the four-lane streets, making green tunnels that are broken by large roundabouts with statues and shrubs and perennially blooming flowers. Life moves at a relaxed and unhurried pace compared to that of her sister river city, Shanghai, 180 miles downstream on the Yangtze.

During five periods in China's history, Nanjing was the national capital (twice in this century). The city of four million people is today the provincial capital of Jiangsu Province.

In the colonial period, Nanjing was bombarded by the British fleet during the Opium War. In 1842 the city fell and the Nanjing Treaty was signed aboard a British gunboat anchored in the harbor. The "unequal" Treaty of Nanjing ceded Hong Kong to the British and granted trading concessions in five cities to the Western colonial powers.

Additional taxes were levied on the already impoverished Chinese peasantry. In response, peasant revolts were endemic, frequent, and intense. The Taiping rebellion began in 1851, and two years later a Tiaping government was set up in Nanjing that controlled south China.

Ten years later, the British interceded to assist the emperor's forces in putting down the Taiping insurrection. The British captured Nanjing (for the second time in a generation) and in three days slaughtered one hundred thousand Taiping soldiers.

In the Taiping campaign, the exploits of a British general, Charles George Gordon, made him an English folk hero, the legendary General "Chinese" Gordon. Both the Nationalists and the Communists would later claim to have their roots in the peasant revolt of Taiping.

One of the darkest chapters in the history of Nanjing occurred in 1938 during the Japanese invasion of China. Nanjing was the capital of Chiang Kaishek's Nationalist government. When the Japanese took the city, the troops went berserk. In an orgy of violence and retribution, the Japanese Army committed the atrocity that history would call "the rape of Nanjing," In a four-day period, forty-four thousand women were raped and one hundred thousand Nanjing civilians murdered.

Over the last four hundred years, China and Japan have gone to war three times. In the war of 1894-1895, China lost Taiwan. In the Japanese invasion of 1937-1945, China lost more than one million dead and almost two million wounded. With the characteristic patience of the Chinese who have always taken the long look, they simply explain their conflicts with Japan as "just a moment" in history.

Today Japan is China's number one trading partner and is engaged in more joint ventures with China than any other country. Japanese make up one third of the tourists now visiting China. The two countries are talking about military cooperation. Such coziness between China and Japan sends shivers down the spine of the Soviets.

The Bridge to Freedom

Today the Yangtze Bridge is Nanjing's most visible claim to fame. However, in the broad sweep of history, when the Yangtze Bridge has long since served its purpose, Nanjing will be remembered as the city where a bridge to freedom was fashioned and the Chinese people began their exodus out of two thousand years of feudal bondage toward the "promised land" of a free people.

It was in Nanjing in October 1911 that the first government of the Republic of China was founded and the first capital of a free China was established. The peasant revolutionary armies had taken most of south China when delegates from seventeen provinces met in Nanjing and elected Dr. Sun Yatsen president of the infant Republic of China. A few months later the Manchu Dynasty collapsed. For the first time in history, the Chinese were a free, self-governing people.

The father of the Republic, Dr. Sun, was born of poor peasant parents in Guangdong Province in 1866. When he was eighteen years old, Sun became a Christian and was baptized by an American missionary. He continued to profess the Christian faith the rest of his life. He spoke of his dream for China, "Our greatest hope is to make the Bible and Christian education as we have come to know them in America and Europe the basis of reform in China,"[2]

Sun received his medical training in Hong Kong. Moved by the plight of the Chinese peasants, Dr. Sun gave up the practice of medicine to become a revolutionary. Exiled by the Manchus for revolutionary activities, Dr. Sun spent much time in the United States, Canada, Europe, and Japan, gathering support for the revolution. He was in Denver, Colorado, when he read in a newspaper that victorious revolutionary forces were sweeping through south China. He rushed home and was elected president of the new republic.

Nanjing became Dr. Sun's favorite city. Here he is buried in a park on the outskirts of the city. The grounds, covering twenty acres, are laid out in the shape of a bell. Three hundred ninety-two granite steps lead up to the imposing mausoleum on the slopes of the pine-forested Purple Hills. In the circular hall is a white marble statue of Dr. Sun, and in the vault below are his remains. On the walls are inscribed Dr. Sun's "Three People's Principles" for leading China into a new age: "Nationalism, Democracy, and Livelihood."

The Ultimate Freedom

Nationalism, democracy, and livelihood—the dream of the Chinese people!

Nationalism! Under Mao, China achieved nationhood. China stood free of foreign domination and achieved a self-identity and national pride.

Livelihood! Under Deng's four modernizations, China is making great strides economically. The infusion of limited capitalism and free enterprise into the Chinese system seems to be working.

Democracy! Whether the motivation is philosophical conviction or pragmatic accommodation, the fact is that giant strides are being taken toward a more open and democratic free society in China. It is nowhere more apparent than in the area of the ultimate freedom, the freedom of religion.

In 1949, the Communist government promised religious freedom to the Chinese people in a single sentence in the constitution. Modeled after the Soviet constitution, it said, "Citizens enjoy the freedom to believe in religion and the freedom not to believe in religion and to propagate atheism." But in Mao's drive to purge Chinese society of all feudal reactionaries and imperialistic foreign domination, this promise was often recklessly ignored. Later, in the Cultural Revolution, there was a ruthless campaign to eradicate religion completely.

A New Promise

Former U.S. president Jimmy Carter recalls his visit with Deng Xiaoping in 1978. "The first evening I spent with Deng, I told him there were three things I wanted him to do. One was to permit Western Christian missionaries to go back into China. The second was to permit the distribution of Bibles. The third was to permit religious freedom."

Deng answered without hesitation, "I will do two of them." Deng said he would do his best to allow complete freedom of religion in China and the distribution of Bibles. But he could not allow missionaries to return because "it puts a connotation of domination by Westerners over the Chinese."

When President Carter visited in a Chinese Protestant church three years later and talked to religious leaders, he observed that Deng "had kept his promises both in spirit and in deed."[3]

The official policy of Deng's new regime was spelled out by Xiao Xianta, director of the government's Religious Affairs Bureau, to the National Islamic Conference meeting in Beijing in April 1980.

Mr. Xiao said, "Allowing religious freedom will help promote the unity of the Chinese people and help rally all segments of Chinese society for China's modernization. There are large numbers of religious believers in China. China needs their loyalty and support." While Communists are theoretically atheists, Xiao went on to say that religious beliefs belong to the ideological sphere, and ideological problems cannot be handled by compulsory measures. Therefore, the policy of the new government under Deng would be that religious believers and atheists are political and social equals in China. No discrimination against religious believers would be permitted.[4]

Three official documents implement the government's new policy toward religion and reflect the breadth of the reforms and the fundamental changes that have been made. The first is a 1982 revision of the constitution. Religious leaders petitioned the government that the constitution was unfair and discriminatory against religious believers and favored atheism by stating that citizens were free to believe or not believe but atheism was "free to teach and propagate." As a result, the constitution was revised to eliminate the reference to atheism's freedom to teach and greatly expanded the provisions guaranteeing religious freedom.

The revised Chapter 2, Article 36 section of the constitution states, "Citizens of the People's Republic of China enjoy freedom of religious belief. No state organ, public organization or individual may compel citizens to believe or not to believe in any religion; nor may they discriminate against the citizens who believe in or do not believe in any religion." The same article goes on to say that "the state protects normal religious activities, which would include public worship, clergy training, publication of scriptures, religious books, journals and training materials."

The second important document is Penal Code 177, which gives new teeth to the enforcement of the constitutional guarantees of religious freedom. The code sets a penalty of up to two years in prison for any official found guilty of denying individuals or groups their religious freedoms or in any way discriminating against persons because of their religious beliefs.

The third statement is an official document on religious freedom, published by the Communist Party Central Committee. It is designed to induce local officials to "implement this policy" and to enforce Penal Code 177 when there are violations. The document declares that the party and the government are obligated to "redress past injustices and violations of religious freedom; provide places for public worship; allow seminaries to train religious leaders; permit religious materials to be published; permit churches to receive donations; to support friendly international relations among religious believers" and many similar statements.[5]

No Illusions

However, Bishop K. H. Ting warns, "We should harbor no illusions about the Communist Party on matters of religious faith. Communists do not have a high regard for religion."[6] The late Southern Baptist Foreign Mission Board executive and former China missionary, Dr. Baker James Cauthen, described the religious freedom of the Chinese as "a horse on a long rope staked out to graze free within limits."[7] Under Deng's administration and with the changes in the constitution and the penal code, the rope has been greatly lengthened. "We never had it so good," a Beijing pastor told me.

But the rope has not been severed. Chinese Christians do not enjoy the absolute freedom that we as Americans are privileged to enjoy. They do have some restrictions. The Communist Party is in full control of society. Party members cannot officially hold religious beliefs or affiliation. Religion is interpreted as a private matter, therefore, individuals are not allowed to distribute publically unapproved religious literature or propagate their religion in public places. Many regional and local municipal officials are contemptuous of religion and resist implementing the constitutional rights of religious citizens. However, more and more, violations of religious freedom are being successfully challenged in the courts of China.

In the central government, Deng's policies are winning. Hong Kong-based Britt E. Towery, Jr., expressed his opinion that "there is no agency in China, today, that is actually anti-religious. With all the catching up they have to do, the government and the party have little time to be promoting atheism and fighting Christians." This is consistent with Deng's modernization policy to bring China into the mainstream of Western nations with a world view on religion and human rights.[8]

Dr. Sun's bridge to freedom, begun in Nanjing in 1911, is being shored up and made stronger by today's bridge builder, Premier Deng Xiaoping.

The Bridge Builder

Another bridge builder with a somewhat similar name, Ding Guangxum, was an engineer on the Yangtze River Bridge project.[9] Ding's vocation was not that of an engineer. He was an Anglican minister. Before 1949, Ding had studied at Columbia University and Union Theological Seminary in New York City. At the beginning of the Cultural Revolution, he was an Anglican minister, theological professor, and president of Jinling Union Seminary.

Ding described what happened when the Red Guards stormed the seminary. "They completely sacked the library, confiscating and destroying 80 percent of the books. They desecrated the chapel and occupied all the facilities. The faculty and ministers were divided into two groups. The first were sent directly to the farms. The others were put under 'house arrest' for reeducation and indoctrination before being sent to the work camps."[10]

However, the Red Guards overextended themselves in their violence in Nanjing, and orders came from Beijing to "draw back." The second group was never sent to the remote countryside. Instead, a room was set aside in the facility and the men were put to work as translators (because of their knowledge of English). They translated the proceedings of the United Nations into Chinese. They produced a dictionary with fifty thousand idioms, phrases, and words from English translated into Chinese. They also translated a number of scientific and technological works into Chinese. Ding was in this second group. Because of some limited engineering training as a young man, he was assigned for a time to the Yangtze project and became a bridge builder.

Bishop Ting

Today Ding is known by his Anglicized name, Bishop K. H. Ting. *Bishop* in Chinese does not signify an office or position. It is a title connotating reverence and high respect. Bishop K. H. Ting has emerged as the paramount leader and spokesman for Chinese Protestant Christianity.

Bishop Ting is a man of high Christian commitment, deep spiritual sensitivities, and courageous leadership. He has been tested and tried by the fires of persecution. Of the sufferings by the Chinese Christians and his own tribulations he said, "Resurrection is the most descriptive word . . . we learned what it is to die and live again. As Paul said, 'We bear in our bodies the death of Jesus Christ.' We have learned that life does not depend on power or wealth, but on the life of Jesus Christ."[11]

Bishop Ting has been a moving force for Christianity in the new China. Ding, the bridge builder, is Bishop Ting, the spiritual engineer, now building bridges of understanding and cooperation.

Nanjing is the present-day organizational hub and center of gravity for the Protestant churches of China. From Nanjing bridges of understanding and cooperation arch out in many directions to establish communication and relationships between Christians, churches, and the government, and the Christian world beyond China.

The Three-Self Patriotic Movement

Bishop Ting has served as chairman of the National Three-Self Patriotic Committee.

Throughout China local Three-Self Committees operate. The concept of self-support, self-control, and self-propagation was initiated in 1950 by the Chinese Christians themselves, not by the Communists. The Three-Self proposal was made by religious leaders to Zhou Enlai to counteract the charge that China and the church were tools of foreign imperialists (as detailed in ch. 2).

The Three-Self Movement is not a church. It has no authority over local congregations, which are autonomous and are managed by the members themselves. The Three-Self Movement is not a government organ. It is an instrument of the churches. The local churches select the members of the Three-Self committees.[12] Three-Self is not the official church of China. There is no official church, as in the state churches of Europe. In China today there are simply four thousand independent Chinese Protestant churches and tens of thousands of free autonomous house churches which cherish their own selfhood and identity as expressed in the Three-Self principles.

On the governmental side is the Religious Affairs Bureau, "set up expressly to handle religious affairs," according to Bishop Ting. It does not deal with the faith, life, and work of the churches. The RAB does not supervise religious activities or exercise any control over the churches. The basic function of the RAB is to implement the policy of religious freedom. The Three-Self Patriotic Movement is the bridge that spans the gap between the church congregations and the government.

From the beginning, the Three-Self Movement has had its detractors.[13] To those who are critical, suspicious, or merely skeptical, Bishop Ting asks that they simply "take the Gamaliel attitude toward it," that is, "if this be of God, it will prosper . . . if not it will die" (see Acts 5:34-39).

Bishop Ting sees the Chinese church setting a pattern for churches in other societies where Nationalism or Socialist society restricts foreign mission activity by Western churches. "Three-Self is an experiment by the Chinese Christians on behalf of the church universal. If it succeeds, it certainly cannot bring harm to Christians elsewhere but can mean their enrichment.

"While we are thankful for all the good that missionaries have done in China," Ting continued, "it was time for weaning and we needed our church to be de-westernized." The divine wisdom of this step is evidenced in the explosion in Christianity that is taking place in China where "Protestant Christianity is growing twice as fast as the population."[14]

A Crooked Path

The Three-Self principle has also been a bridge to unify on a common ground the churches of China, which were badly fragmented by denominational divisions.

Denominationalism was always a cause of confusion and conflict in China, as on many other mission fields. "We walked a crooked path trying to selectively uphold . . . denominational differences that were completely foreign," says Ms. Tsao Sangchiah. Foreign mission societies, through comity agreements, divided China into spheres of influence and work. For example, Northern Baptists took south China while Southern Baptists had north China. It was very confusing. "Baptists in Southern China were called 'Northern Baptists' while those in the North were 'Southern Baptist.'"[15]

In Shanghai, Baptists were divided into two associations, the Mandarin-speaking and the Shanghai-dialect churches. This was not because the Chinese could not understand each other, but the American missionaries who worked with the churches were not trained in both dialects. This simply reinforced the image that the church was a Western institution and Christianity a foreign religion.[16]

In Hangzhou (Hangchow) there were twenty-three churches sponsored by eight different mission societies and denominations. One pastor told me, "We had no 'Reformation' as did Europe, or 'Civil War' as did America. But the missionaries who came to us were very subjective, bringing all the divisions of Protestantism that your history dictated. We didn't have the same 'history' and sought the biblical idea of 'one Lord, one faith, one baptism.'"

Bishop K. H. Ting commented on the belief of the Anglican Church in apostolic succession. "This may be very important to the Archbishop of Canterbury, but not to the Chinese Anglicans" who are concerned with building the church of Christ in China.[17]

Britt E. Towery, Jr., China liaison director for the Cooperative Services International in Hong Kong, cautioned, "We must overcome the colonial missionary mentality of wanting to make the church of China in our own Western image. It will be a serious mistake if we pass judgment on the Chinese churches from our own narrow denominational perspectives."[18]

Postdenominationalism

"The Chinese church has advanced into the postdenominational era," Mr. Li Shou-bao told me. "We are Three-Self in practice, but part of the church universal in faith. We give freedom to each church to set its own form of worship. Within the church, we have mutual respect for those who differ in practice on such matters as baptism and communion. For example, each individual may choose the mode of baptism, either by sprinkling or immersion."[19]

The Christians of China really did not fully move into this post-denominational relationship until after the sufferings of the Cultural Revolution. One pastor who survived the terror of that decade said, "We worked and ate together. We wept and laughed together. We grew to-gether. Suffering brought us close to God and to the realities of life."[20]

The YMCA

"The YMCA is a bridge," Li Shou-bao, general secretary of the YMCA of China, told me.

The YMCA was a strong influence in the early days of the Christian missionary movement in China. Premier Zhou Enlai and his wife, in their younger years, were members of the YMCA and YWCA. The movement was popular because of the social ministry aspects, recreation, sports, club and social events, and language and self-improvement courses.

"The YMCA in China emphasizes two things," Mr. Li told me. "First is the C. We are unapologetically Christian in belief, practice, and program. This is different from your American organization which has lost its Christian emphasis and identification. If we do not keep this distinctive, we do not need to exist. There are so many other youth organizations in China which can do purely social work."

The second distinctive is that the YMCA is not an exclusive body for Christian only. "We reach out to all youth and adults of all faiths or none. A Communist, Moslem, Buddhist, anyone can join a YMCA language class. Historically this approach of service to all the society has created a good image for Christianity with the public and the Communist Party. The YMCA is strong in China today."

"The YMCA is desperately needed today in China," Mr. Kao Yung-chung told me. He is a deacon in Guangzhou's Dongshan Church and associate secretary of the YMCA.

Deng's policy of socialist-capitalism brought an exploding prosperity to the new China. Today workers are fired for nonperformance, variable wages are tied directly to production, and free markets operate with attendant risks of loss.

These almost unthinkable innovations for a Communist system have produced the other side of the coin of free enterprise: unemployment, economic inequity, crime, and violence. So Mr. Kao said, "There are many unemployed young men in China creating serious problems for our society. The YMCA, through Christian activities, recreation, training, and social programs, can bear a witness to Christ."

The general secretary, Mr. Li, said, "The YMCA is a bridge, creating understanding between the government and the church. Then, gradually, the Church will stand on its own feet, accepted by the government and the Chinese people and free to function in these areas."

The China Christian Council

The China Christian Council is yet another bridge that links the scattered churches of China together to accomplish cooperatively what they cannot do individually. "The CCC exists to aid and serve the churches and in no way exercises control over the churches," Mr. Han Wenzao, the associate general secretary, told me. The CCC functions in three major areas.

First, the CCC represents the churches whenever there are violations of religious freedom by local governments, officials, or individuals. Second, the CCC is responsible for theological education and operates the Protestant seminaries for the churches and develops training programs for the laity. Third, the CCC publishes Bibles, hymnals, and literature, as requested and required by the churches.

Theological Education

"Our emphasis the first three years, beginning in 1979, was to reopen the churches," Han told me. "Since then we have been majoring on training. Churches are growing so rapidly and there is a great shortage of trained leadership."

At the present time eleven Protestant seminaries are in full operation in China, Jinling Union Seminary in Nanjing and ten regional seminaries.

To qualify for admission, a candidate must:

1. Be an active Christian affiliated with a church;
2. Be a graduate from a senior secondary school and under twenty-five years of age;
3. Take an entrance examination; and
4. Have a letter of recommendation from his or her home church.

Candidates are accepted for a two-year course in theological and pastoral training. The best-qualified students may take an additional two-year course which leads to a Bachelor of Theology degree.

Ten or more people apply for each vacancy. High priority is given to the recommendation of the local church, and all applicants must be cleared by local church authorities before being considered by the seminary's admissions committee.[21]

Training of Laity

The CCC recognized the impossible task of producing enough seminary-trained pastors for the more than four thousand open churches and the tens of thousands of house churches. Therefore, the seminary developed the Leadership Training Correspondence Course for pastors.

"Our first objective was to enroll two hundred students," Mr. Han said. "We designed a syllabus of study and set up a procedure for papers to be mailed back to the seminary, graded, and credit given. When we offered the course, forty thousand people enrolled. We had neither the personnel nor the money to carry out our original program.

"God turned us in another direction," Han said. "What China really needed was a simple Bible study correspondence course for lay leadership. Now we are training forty thousand believers from all walks of life who are preaching and teaching in thousands of meeting points throughout China."

"We could never train enough pastors to do the work they do," a seminary professor in Nanjing told me.

The China Christian Council has also published a series of six booklets for short-term, on-site training courses in the churches. The courses are Introduction to the Old and New Testaments, Study of 1 and 2 Corinthians, How to Be a Pastor, Homiletics, and Basic Teachings of Christianity.

The need for trained leadership is great. For example, in a county near Nanjing, large congregations gather at twenty-six meeting points. There are only seven trained evangelists (or preachers). At the remaining nineteen locations, Christians gather for prayer services with no sermons because no one feels competent to preach.[22]

Bible Production

"That is the reason the China Christian Council is also majoring on Bible publication," Han Wenzao told me. Since 1980, 2.1 million Bibles have been printed in China, plus 750,000 New Testaments, a new hymnal, and many other pieces of Christian literature.

The China Christian Council has also printed Bibles in three minority languages—Korean, Miao, and Lisu.

A 7.2 million dollar state-of-the-art printing press, computerized typesetter, and high-speed bindery are being installed in Nanjing. This is a partnership project between the United Bible Societies of the world and Chinese Christians. The high-speed press is expected to turn out 750,000 Bibles and New Testaments a year, in addition to hymnals and other Christian literature. The Chinese government encouraged the project by allowing the machinery to enter duty free.

The United Bible Societies is composed of 102 affiliated societies of the world. "This is the largest single project the United Bible Societies have ever undertaken," Leland Waggoner, a trustee of the executive committee of the American Bible Society, told me.

Three factors contributed to the need for decisive action. First was the burgeoning printing demands of China. Her exploding modernization program is taxing the present printing facilities for priority items. That is why the Chinese churches had to have a printing press of their own. Because of a critical shortage of printing machinery and paper, most books published in China today are issued in very small editions of perhaps ten thousand to twenty thousand copies. Popular English textbooks or Chinese-English dictionaries are sold out in a few hours. This makes the publication of Bibles, not in quantities of ten thousand but over two million, most significant!

A second factor is the great demand from the believers for Bibles in the many open churches and household congregations. Third, there is also a great demand for Bibles among nonbelievers, especially university students.

Stories abound of the Chinese people's curiosity about the Bible. Professor C. K. Chang told me of his neighbor, the retiring president of the university, who said, "I am an atheist. But now that I have the time, I would like a Bible to read so I can learn all about it."

Leland Waggoner told me of the riverboat captain on a Yangtze River Gorge cruise who came to his cabin and said, "My brother-in-law has a Bible. I love the stories in it, especially the one about the shepherd boy killing the giant. Do you have a Bible I could have to read?"

The two young soldiers asked my traveling companion, John Wood, for Bibles, and the university student in the Forbidden City . . . the list is endless.

A Bridge Over Troubled Waters

"There is no doubt that the major link that holds Chinese Protestant Christians together is the common Bible," says Dr. Hans Reudi-Weber.[23]

When the Cultural Revolution began, Bibles were declared to be poisonous literature and were confiscated and burned by the Red Guards whenever found. During the ten years that followed, Bibles became almost nonexistent in China. One pastor told me that his family managed to keep a copy hidden behind a movable stone in an outdoor oven. Everywhere throughout China, Bibles became rare and treasured items. Some were secretly reproduced by mimeograph. Han Wenzao told of a mimeographed copy he had seen, beautifully decorated. Other people managed to have portions of Scripture secreted away that were brought out for private family devotionals. Another eighty-five-year-old saint recalled this dark period, "I had no Bible, but I read it from my memory."

The 1986 calendar published by the China Christian Council pictures an elderly Chinese man clutching a Bible to his heart. Across the bottom are the words of Jeremiah 15:16 written in Chinese, "Your words fill my heart with joy and gladness." The Word of God is a bridge over troubled waters for the heart that believes.

Notes

1. Personal interview with Dr. C. K. Chang, professor of English, Anhui Normal University of Wuhu, PRC.

2. Editorial, "Christianity in China," *Christian Science Monitor*, December 26, 1979, p. 12.

3. Clay Brown, "Carter Reveals Private Talk with Chinese Leader," *Western Recorder*, June 26, 1984, p. 1.

4. Xiao Xiania, "Equality for Chinese Believers," *China Daily*, April 18, 1980, p. 3.

5. Document 19, entitled "The Basic Viewpoint and Policy on the Religious Question During Our Country's Socialist Period," has been translated by Janice Wickeri, Tao Fong Shan Ecumenical Center, and published in Hong Kong in 1984.

6. Bishop K. H. Ting, "The Policy of Religious Freedom," *China Notes*, Winter 1980-1981, p. 146.

7. Dr. Baker James Cauthen in a Baptist Press release, June 11, 1980.

8. Britt E. Towery, Jr., *The Churches of China* (Hong Kong: Amazing Grace Books, Ltd. 1986), p. 3.

9. Ibid., Ch. 2, p. 15.

10. Leland Waggoner, chief executive officer of the Virginia Life Insurance Company of New York and member of the executive committee of the American Bible Society, related these details to me as we were traveling on a train from Nanjing to Shanghai. He had been at dinner with Bishop Ting in his home two nights earlier.

11. Towery, Ch. 9, p. 15.

12. Ibid., Ch. 9, p. 19.

13. In the beginning, the most notable critic of the Three-Self Patriotic Movement was popular evangelist Wang Mingdao, who charged that TSPM was a Communist plot to subvert the churches. Today the opposition is centered largely in Hong Kong among the overseas Chinese. This opposition is somewhat understandable in that it is rooted in a complex set of bitter memories of past sufferings and present emotions that are anti-Communist, pro-Taiwan, and anti-anything connected with the People's Republic of China, including the churches of China. This opposition is exploited to raise funds for so-called "Bible smuggling" operations based in Europe and the United States.

14. Towery, Ch. 10.

15. Yap Kin Hao, "The Christian Conference of Asia," *China Notes*, Spring/Summer, 1981, p. 159.

16. Dr. C. K. Chang, a minister and former professor at Shanghai University, told me how he finally led the two associations to unite in the fall of 1948, just one year before liberation.

17. Alf Lohne, "China Report," *Ministry*, September 1980, p. 2.

18. In a personal interview with Britt E. Towery, Jr., in Hong Kong.

19. Personal interview with Mr. Li Shou-bao, general secretary of the National Committee of the YMCA of China, in Shanghai.

20. Towery, p. 49.

21. Deng Zhao Ming, "How Jingling Theological Seminary Recruits Students," *Bridge*, July 1984, 6:6-7.

22. Ibid. p. 8.

23. Hans Reudi-Weber, "The Bible as the Key Link," *The Bridge*, July 1984, 6:14-16.

10

The Time of the Dragon

The time is 1957. The place is Nanjing, China. Eight years have passed since the foreign missionaries left China. The Chinese Christians have regrouped under Chinese leadership in churches that are tolerated by the new government.

On Tien'anmen Square in Beijing stand the giant portraits of the prophets of a new religion: Karl Marx, Friedrich Engels, Joseph Stalin, and Mao Zedong. Communism is the new philosophy and atheism the new faith. Karl Marx had called religion "the opium of the people." Friedrich Engels had written, "All religion is none other than an illusory reflection in the mind of man of the external forces that dominate him in his everyday life. In this reflection, human forces take the form of superhuman forces." Mao Zedong had declared, "Man makes religion, religion does not make man. The people cannot be really happy until it has been deprived of illusory happiness by the abolition of religion."[1]

Atheism captures the minds of the young people and relentlessly begins to devour the land. Church attendance and support declines everywhere throughout China, and Christians continue to be under suspicion because of their adherence to a foreign faith.

Now the Christian community faces a new crisis. Mao Zedong tightens the screws on religion as he launches his "great leap forward." Churches everywhere are being closed and appropriated for the "constructive" use of the people, and the congregations are being consolidated. The society is progressing toward the avowed goal of the complete eradication of the superstition called "religion."

At a gathering of Christian leaders in Nanjing, Dr. K. H. Ting, the

principal of Jinling Union Theological Seminary (which is still in operation), addresses the group.

"The establishment of the church in a socialist society is the task that
was never accomplished in all the 19 centuries of church history. Why
did the Lord give these duties to us? The Chinese churches are weak
without antecedent prestige," Ting says. True! The small, independent
Chinese churches, self-supporting, self-controlled, and self-
propagating, stand alone. They are completely cut off from all worldwide denomination structures and support systems. They have no
outside financial resources. They are without an advocate in the circles
of international diplomacy.

Bishop Ting continues, "But the Lord has his own purpose, one we
cannot fathom. The Lord in weakness shows forth strength. God has
indeed chosen the foolish things of the world to put to shame those that
are strong, to show that the strength is from God and not from ourselves."[2]

As Bishop Ting speaks, the Christian leaders never dream that the
worst is yet to come. In nine years the Cultural Revolution will close
every church in China, and public evidence of Christianity in any form
will completely disappear for almost a decade.

The Resurrection

Mao died. The ultra-leftist extremes were purged. Deng Xiaoping
took the helm, and a new era began for China. Bishop Ting's prophecy
of God's triumph began to be miraculously fulfilled, which Ting described as nothing less than a "resurrection."

In 1979, like spring flowers breaking forth on an alpine meadow after
a long bitter winter, the "resurrected" churches of China began to ap-
pear, first in Zhenjiang Province of East China at Ningbo City, then in
Shanghai, then in Guangzhou (Canton), and after that all over the land.
By 1986 there were four thousand resurrected Protestant churches in
China with a membership of over four million. This is more than five
times the number of church members in all the Protestant churches of
China in 1949.

These resurrected churches were seeded in the 150 years of foreign missionary efforts. They were nurtured and made strong by the Three-Self principles during almost thirty years of persecution. Now post-denominational, the emerging churches are reclaiming the buildings of the denominational era and reopening as authentic, dynamic, indigenous Chinese churches effectively operating and growing in a Socialist society.

These open, organized churches are sometimes erroneously called the official or authorized government-controlled churches. While the churches are regulated by certain restrictions, they are not the government's official church; nor are the leaders or the members controlled by the government. The Three-Self principles apply inside China as well as outside China. Their churches are simply independent congregations.

The Spontaneous Church

In addition to the organized reopened churches, there are the house churches of China which more appropriately could now be called home gatherings or meeting places. These are spontaneous churches. They came from volunteer seed, scattered by a multitude of unknown circumstances and unnamed sowers and germinated by the spirit of God. These are free, independent, unstructured groups.

The spontaneous churches have in times past met secretly; but now, openly. They may meet in large groups outdoors in fields or in smaller groups in halls, warehouses, or homes.

The leaders of the spontaneous church usually emerge from within the group. The leadership is unordained and largely self-trained. This spontaneous church is usually very zealous, pietistic, and emotional.

As has been already indicated, the number of Christian believers in these tens of thousands of spontaneous churches in China has been estimated to be twenty-five million. Rapid growth continues.

Han Wenzao told me, "Some people think there are two Protestant churches in China, an 'official' government Three-Self church that is Communist-controlled and the 'underground' house churches which they think are really the 'true' New Testament churches. This is completely inaccurate. The open churches are not controlled by the Communists; neither are the house churches an underground resistance movement against the government or a protest group against the open churches." My experiences in China have confirmed the truth of Han's statement.

The first house churches of China were strictly family churches that gathered for prayer, Bible study, singing, and worship in the privacy of the home. During the ten years of the Cultural Revolution, this was the only church that existed in China. This private expression of faith is still preferred by some because of the intimacy of the fellowship and the opportunity for individual participation. Many of the larger, open, spontaneous groups have sprung up from these small family house churches.

The Chinese Christians have not only built indigenous churches in a socialist society but have also challenged atheism head-on. "Christians must learn to live with atheists, not being seduced by them but learning how to present the gospel to them," Bishop Ting declared. "While Christian belief is not the result of reasoning but of experience, believers must be able to present the cause of Christ intelligently and persuasively." The strategy is to "turn the tables on the issues and the questions of the atheists," Ting said. "Ask them, Why do you not believe in God?" Actually to refuse to believe in God is the real opiate. "How many men since the beginning of history have drugged themselves by the denial of God's existence so they could continue to sin, avoid responsibility for their actions, and stifle the reproaches of conscience?" Belief in God makes great demands on people's lives, on their thinking and actions. "Atheism is but an attempt to escape from these moral responsibilities."[3]

A Clever Plot?

The Chinese religious leaders I have talked with genuinely believe in the government's policy of democratic socialism along with the capitalistic twist that Deng has applied. Most believe that the average citizen's condition has improved considerably and that China is a more just society today than it was before 1949. All have glowing praise for the government's new policies of religious freedom.

But some critics abroad suggest that the churches are being used by the government. They charge that this newly granted religious freedom is but a pragmatic move, a clever plot, to help build a united China and achieve Deng's modernization goals that would be impossible to reach without the support of the religious communities of China.

One may ask, Are the churches of China compromising the gospel by contributing to the unification of Chinese society as it seeks to achieve materialistic and nationalistic goals? Two answers may be given to this question. First, the end result is that the door has been opened for the preaching of the gospel, which is the "power of God unto salvation" (Rom. 1:16). Ulterior motives on the part of the government leaders do not invalidate the goodness of the gospel opportunity that develops from these bad motives.

Dr. Bryant Hicks, professor of missions at The Southern Baptist Theological Seminary of Louisville, Kentucky, uses the example of the present-day explosion of Christianity in Korea. He believes that the foundation for the phenomenal growth of Christianity in Korea today was laid a decade ago when the Korean government required every soldier to affirm some religion. With superficial and insincere motives, many soldiers arbitrarily selected Christianity. But in so doing, they, their families, and their children began to be exposed to the power of the gospel. A genuine revival occurred, first in the army and now in the country as a whole, as the power of God was released.

The second aspect of this question deals with the role of the church in joining with the government to build a better China. Is this wrong? Does this compromise the church?

Perhaps we should address this question to ourselves and our American churches. Is it a compromise for the church to encourage economic progress for the community and the country, to advocate decency and morality, to challenge church members to be good hardworking citizens? Is it wrong for churches to call upon believers to obey the law?

There is a distinction between love for China and the support of Communism. Chinese Christians love their country and support the government programs that advance education, health care, and human rights but do not endorse the many tenets of Communism.

Britt Towery, who has visited extensively in churches throughout

China, told me that he had never seen a Communist banner or the flag of China in a Chinese church sanctuary. But in America, in many churches, the pulpit is flanked by the American flag and the Christian flag. Is the expression of patriotism and love for our country a compromise for American Christians? Is love for the motherland a compromise for the Chinese Christians?

Bishop K. H. Ting comes through loud and clear on the basic issue. "The first loyalty of the Chinese church is to Christ. At this time there is no conflict between the church and the government."[4]

Chinese church leaders and Chinese believers are neither secret atheists nor clandestine Communists. They are fellow believers and followers of our Lord, our brothers and sisters in Christ.

What About Missionaries?

The most frequently asked question about China in Christian circles today is, When can we send missionaries again? As is already evident in everything I have reported, the answer is, Not anytime in the foreseeable future.

The real question is not *can we* but *should we* send missionaries? Given all the dynamics in China today, economic, governmental, and religious, would the presence of foreign missionaries serving in the traditional manner be helpful? Would a foreign missionary presence in China erode the Three-Self Chineseness of the churches, a factor that has been one of the dynamics that accounts for their spectacular growth? Are there other Christian approaches to China that would be more fruitful than "foreign missionaries"?

The door to an individual Christian's involvement in China is not closed. Deng's principles of economic reform that provided for joint ventures between Chinese and foreign businesses have been extended to the health, education, and social welfare field. While Christians can no longer go as missionaries, preachers, or evangelists, China gladly welcomes individuals who have skills or technical training that China needs and are willing to come and help the Chinese people. There is a great need for agricultural experts, public health and social workers, teachers (especially English), business experts, and doctors.

AMITY

Many foreign Christians are now working in China, and funds and materials are being sent by religious and benevolent groups for the first time in thirty-five years. Pioneering in this development is the Chinese-Christian-initiated AMITY Foundation. AMITY is the combination of two Chinese words that mean *love* and *virtue*. Han Wenzao is the general secretary.

"The purpose of AMITY is to make our Christian presence felt in China," Han told me. "The personal witness is still the most effective way of doing evangelism in our country. Many Chinese say that Christians are very strange, dangerous, foreign-influenced persons. But through AMITY we can show that they are honest, caring persons doing their best to meet human needs. This will lay the foundations for broader and more open opportunities later." AMITY serves as a channel for the ecumenical sharing of resources and international people-to-people relationships. Initial accomplishments have included teacher recruitment, establishing of a Bible printing facility, and numerous medical, health, and nutritional projects.

A similar foundation, the Love Social Service Center, appealing especially to overseas Chinese Christians, has been established in Guangzhou.

Many major denominations are either working directly with AMITY or have established special divisions to develop and coordinate partnership social and educational projects.

The Cooperative Services Foundation (a Southern Baptist agency) with Britt E. Towery, Jr., as liaison director, operates in Hong Kong as a "friendship bridge" facilitating partnership projects in education, health care, food production, and other humanitarian projects.

The Educational Exchange (an inter-Mennonite organization) sponsors exchanges of agriculturalists, nurses, and doctors.

A fuller listing of the other Protestant denominations involved in China partnership ministries is given in the Appendix.

A number of institutions are directly engaged in joint-services projects with Chinese institutions. These are but a few examples:

Baylor University of Waco, Texas, is working in Beijing with the Second Foreign Language Institute in an exchange of professors; in Kunming in the University of Nationalities working with minorities; in Shanghai working with the Institute of Mechanical Engineering; in Henan Province where the Baylor School of Nursing is linked with the provincial medical school developing a graduate nursing degree program.

Grand Canyon College of Phoenix, Arizona, is working in Xinjiang Province. Two agricultural consultants are teaching in the college at Urumqi and conducting a summer student-exchange program.

Bowman Gray Medical School of Winston-Salem, North Carolina, is engaged in several joint projects whereby doctors and medical personnel work with hospitals in various Chinese cities. Samford University of Birmingham, Alabama, is working with Anhui University in Wuhu, China. Jacksonville Baptist Medical Center has a joint relationship with the Drum Tower Hospital in Nanjing.

While it is clearly emphasized that these exchanges are not to be interpreted as mission projects and are not in violation of the autonomony and selfhood of the Chinese churches, it is very clear that Christian teachers, doctors, technicians, and other volunteers are working, witnessing, living, and practicing their faith openly in China and are there at the invitation of the Chinese.

The Scattered Ones

Surely this approach is God's open door to China today. While a concerned Christian cannot go as a "foreign missionary," China invites anyone, including Christians, to "come help us build a better China and help the Chinese people. As you work, you may freely attend church, practice your faith, and share your witness as a Christian in a personal and private way with anyone who is interested."

In fact, I was told that Christians are actually preferred. Recently there was an official request for three hundred English teachers. Unofficially they requested "Christians, if possible." The Chinese have found that Christians are more compassionate, more sensitive to human need, moral, dedicated, with a life-style more acceptable to the Chinese.

One Christian Chinese educator told me, "Please urge your fellow

Christians to come help us. We are getting too many of the 'other' kind, young people who are here just for an overseas travel experience, graduate students interested only in gathering material for a dissertation or a book, or others who are misfits. Christians are 'different.'"

The door is also open for the sharing of funds and resources. Bishop Ting said, "We welcome funds, materials, and personnel from overseas, provided that they are given with due regard to Chinese national sovereignty . . . as expressions of Christian love and care . . . not presented as a 'return to the past missionary era.'" Such help is accepted as an expression of Christian love from abroad and as evidence of the universality of the Christian faith.[5]

In practice, the door is wide open in China today. By identifying with the needs and the ambitions of the Chinese people in building a new China, Christians can go in as partners and fellow workers in achieving their humanitarian and social goals.

There are opportunities for joint ventures in business and manufacturing. China is open for small factories, technicians, and professional engineers. Warmhearted Christians can enter into these joint ventures to legitimately do business and frequently have the opportunity to bear a witness through their life-style and through personal contacts with individual Chinese people.

The New Testament tells how the early Christians "were scattered abroad [and] went every where witnessing" (Acts 8:4). That early church was scattered by persecution. As they went, they planted the seed of the gospel and little colonies of believers sprang up all over the Roman Empire and became churches.

In this day, Christians are scattered throughout the world by international travel, tourism, overseas business enterprises, and cultural exchanges. China, and this world, could be won to Christ if, as in the New Testament era, every "scattered one" became a living witness. Professional missionaries and ordained religionists alone are not sufficient to get the global task done.

Students

Yet another wide-open door to the world is through foreign students enrolled in American colleges and universities.

In a recent study conducted by Benton Williams, it was revealed that chief executives of 210 nations of the world have studied in the United States. That means that we have had access to the leaders of the nations of the world who at some time in their lives were students living in the very community where we have Christian churches and church youth ministries.

Regarding China, ever since 1979 there has been an increasing stream of children of the party elite coming to the United States to study. Fox Butterfield cites some examples. One of Deng's sons, a physicist, was a graduate student at the University of Rochester. Deng's daughter lived in the Chinese embassy in Washington where her husband was a military attache. The son of the foreign minister, Huang Hua, was an undergraduate at Harvard. The daughter of Liu Shaoqi, the late head of state, was enrolled at Boston University. Dozens of offspring of politburo members and cabinet ministers are now in the United States.[6]

More than ten thousand Mainland Chinese are now studying in the United States, offering Christian families the opportunity to cultivate these students, become their "adopted" family, help them at times of need, and bring them under the influence of a Christian life-style. One Christian family set about to cultivate a dozen Chinese students in a local university in this manner. Three of the twelve were won to Christ. Two are going back as medical doctors to China.[7]

Not By Bread Alone

The foreign missionary era of China appears to have ended. Nevertheless, the door is open to the gospel and to Christlike believers who are willing to bear a Christian witness through humanitarian service to the masses of China.

My optimism about the ultimate victory of Christianity over atheism in China is based on the apostle Paul's apologetic on Mars Hill (Acts 17). All human beings are instinctively religious. If they cannot know the true God, they make their own god to worship. But these false gods never satisfy the nameless longing and gnawing hearthunger as they quest after the true God.

I have seen the hungry heart of China, the emptiness of materialistic atheism, and the validation of the truth that "man shall not live by bread alone."

A medical student to whom I gave a Bible said, "I have been educated, like most Chinese youth, to believe in atheism. I was a pious believer in Marxism. The Cultural Revolution smashed that ideal in my mind. Now I refuse to believe anything except what I have seen myself. My father, who was a Christian before liberation, told me that if all the books in the world were to be destroyed except two, he would choose to have the Holy Bible and Shakespeare. If only one, he would choose the Bible. Now you have given me a Bible. It will be useful for making me a better human being and making this a better world and will help me to know that there is a God and will give me something I can believe in."

At Nanjing University one thousand students showed up for the first academic lecture on Christianity. A young woman wrote the *China Youth* magazine, reflecting the emptiness of official atheism. "Life, is this the mystery you try to reveal? Is the ultimate end nothing more than a dead body?" When the letter was published, it drew sixty thousand other letters in response, echoing the same sense of futility and asking the same question.[8]

A university professor told me, "My son is a forty-year-old Communist. He is disillusioned now. He says that the Communists say one day 'this is right,' but the next day they say, 'the same thing is wrong.' One day it is 'black,' the next day it is 'white.' We cannot live like this. We must have something more eternal and fixed. There must be something that controls the affairs of humanity. I find the young people on the campuses of China expressing this same yearning for a spiritual interpretation of life. They hunger for stability, for some eternal truths, for an anchor in life. They are ready for the Gospel of Christ! They are ready for something to give meaning to life and importance to individual human beings."[9]

Moses P. G. Xie, a pastor of the Flower Lane Church in Fuzhou, said, "People are demanding longer sermons and deeper sermons on religion and faith. One-third of the congregation is young people."

The Time of the Dragon

"Does not the Bible say, 'The Lord is not willing that any should perish, but that all should come to repentance'?" (2 Pet. 3:9) a Chinese pastor asked me! "Surely this means that it is God's purpose that the world's largest nation of people, over a billion, should not perish, but be saved, now." With great excitement he continued, "When I was a professor at Shanghai University before liberation, I taught my students how God prepared and used the crosscurrents of history in the Roman world to prepare for the coming of Christ.

"Today China is similar to the world at the time of the birth of Christ. We have one universal language, Mandarin, for the first time in our history. The roads are open for travel and commerce. Chinese bandits that from antiquity plagued the remote areas have been eradicated. There is political stability, a strong central government, and peace throughout the empire. There is a great spiritual vacuum as the ancient traditional religions have been rejected. It is the time of the dragon for the coming of the Lamb.

"The Bible says that '[in] the fulness of the time . . . God sent forth his Son' (Gal. 4:4). This means that in God's divine purpose he had perfectly prepared the world to receive the Savior and the time of his advent had come. We Chinese believe that God has now prepared our world to receive His Son. It is God's 'fullness of time' for China."

Notes

1. George N. Patterson, *Christianity in Communist China* (Waco: Word, 1969), p. xii.

2. Bishop K. H. Ting, "A Message from Chinese Christians to Mission Boards Abroad," Documents of the Three Self Movement, Francis P. Jones, ed. and trans. (New York: National Council of Churches, East Asia Department, 1963) pp. 156-167.

3. Ibid.

4. Glen Douglas, "The Tianjin Conference: Evangelicals and the TSPM," *China and the Church Today*, February 1985, 7,1:13.

5. *Bridge*, January-February 1986, p. 3, article by Philip L. Wickeri.

6. Fox Butterfield, *China, Alive in the Bitter Sea* (New York: Bantam Books, 1982), p. 38.

7. Lewis Myers of Richmond, Virginia, tells of this family.

8. Richard N. Ostling, "Let a Hundred Churches Bloom," *Time* Magazine, May 4, 1981, p. 55.

9. Personal interview with Dr. C. K. Chang.

Appendix

**Some Church Groups Presently Having Cooperative Relations with Churches,
Social Service Organizations, Medical and Educational
Institutions in the People's Republic of China
With a Brief Statement of the Nature of Involvement**

These organizations and denominations do not sponsor missionaries or engage in independent evangelistic activity in China. They respect the "Three-Self" principles of the churches and are supportive of the Christian endeavors of Chinese believers in connection with the China Christian Council and the AMITY Foundation. They seek to contribute to the building of the New China through partnerships in education, health care, food production, and other humanitarian projects by sharing personnel, liaison, consultations, and funding in response to "need" requests initiated by the Chinese.

The American Baptist Churches, P.O. Box 851, Valley Forge, PA 19482. "Working with the China Christian Council through the American Baptist's International Ministries Board . . . direct involvement includes enlisting teachers and funding for disaster relief." Dr. Cecil E. Carder, Area Secretary, Southeast Asia/China.

The American Lutheran Church, 422 South Fifth Street, Minneapolis, Man 55415. "Working through an educational foundation . . . supporting English teachers, and maintaining direct relationships with a Chinese University." Dr. Mark Thomsen, director of World Mission and Inter-Church Cooperation.

Church of the Brethren, 1451 Dundee Avenue, Elgin, IL 60120. Involved in "an exchange program: providing English teachers and agricultural scientists." Dr. J. Roger Schrock, World Ministries Commission Executive.

Christian Church (Disciples of Christ), P.O. Box 1986, Indianapolis, IN 46206. Involved in "supporting volunteer teachers in China and participation in the publication of the *Bridge* Magazine." Dr. Robert S. Bates, Executive Secretary for the Department of East Asia, Overseas Ministries.

Lutheran Church in America, 233 Madison Avenue, New York, NY 10016. "Have provided teachers . . . and participated in providing a new printing press." Dr. Gerald E. Currens, Executive Director for the Division of World Missions and Ecumenism.

National Council of Churches, 475 Riverside Drive, New York, NY 10115. "East Asia/Pacific Division coordinates ecumenical work of American bodies." Publishes *China Notes*.

The Southern Baptist Convention works through **Cooperative Services International,** Dr. Lewis I. Myers, Secretary, P.O. Box 6597, Richmond, VA 23230. Work in the PRC is through the **Cooperative Services Foundation China Liaison Office,** Britt E. Towery, Jr., director. "CSF coordinates joint projects in the fields of Education, Social Services, medical and public health by recruiting professionals . . . teachers, agricultural experts and medical personnel are working in Chinese universities and hospitals." Publishes the *China Journal* and *The Realm of Reality*.

United Church of Christ, 475 Riverside Drive, 16th Floor, New York, NY 10115. "Involvement includes English teachers, disaster relief and scholarship grants for the training of Chinese scholars in America and elsewhere." Publishes *China Talk* through the **Hong Kong China Liaison Office of the General Board of Global Ministries**, #2 Man Wan Rd. C-17, Kowloon, Hong Kong. Dr. Ching-fen Hsiao, East Asia Secretary.

The Wesleyan Church, P.O. Box 2000, Marion, IN 46952. "Shared in the joint Bible Societies printing press project." Dr. Wayne W. Wright.

Other Addresses and Publications

The AMITY Foundation, 17 Da Jian Yin Xiang, Nanjing, People's Republic of China. Publishes the *AMITY Newsletter.*

The Bridge, reporting on Protestant Christianity in China, published monthly by the Tao Fong Shan Ecumenical Centre, Tao Fong Shan Road, Shatin, N.T., Hong Kong.

China Daily, an English-language daily newspaper published in Beijing. North American edition published by *China Daily,* 15 Mercer St., New York, NY 10013.

China Reconstructs, a monthly English language magazine reporting on developments in the People's Republic of China, Wai Wen Building, Beijing (37), China. U.S. $12 per year.

Love Service Center, Dong Shan Church, 9 Sibei Tong Jin, Dong Shan District, Guangzhou, People's Republic of China.